All About Panama Canal: A Kid's Guide to Engineering's Greatest Shortcut

Educational Books For Kids, Volume 40

Shah Rukh

Published by Shah Rukh, 2024.

While every precaution has been taken in the preparation of this book, the publisher assumes no responsibility for errors or omissions, or for damages resulting from the use of the information contained herein.

ALL ABOUT PANAMA CANAL: A KID'S GUIDE TO ENGINEERING'S GREATEST SHORTCUT

First edition. October 27, 2024.

ISBN: 979-8227296696

Written by Shah Rukh.

Table of Contents

Prologue..1

Chapter 1: The Story Behind the Panama Canal....................2

Chapter 2: How the Panama Canal Was Built.......................6

Chapter 3: Digging Through Mountains and Jungles 11

Chapter 4: The Incredible Locks of the Panama Canal.................16

Chapter 5: Meet Ferdinand de Lesseps: The Canal Dreamer 20

Chapter 6: How Ships Travel Through the Canal......................24

Chapter 7: The Challenges of Building the Canal.....................28

Chapter 8: The Role of Teddy Roosevelt in the Panama Canal....33

Chapter 9: Life in the Panama Canal Zone 38

Chapter 10: The French Effort to Build the Canal 42

Chapter 11: The Importance of the Panama Canal Today 47

Chapter 12: How the Panama Canal Changed Global Trade 52

Chapter 13: Animals and Nature Around the Canal 57

Chapter 14: The Technology Behind the Canal's Locks...............62

Chapter 15: The Workers Who Built the Panama Canal 67

Chapter 16: The Expansion of the Panama Canal....................72

Chapter 17: Life in Panama Before the Canal........................78

Chapter 18: The Engineering Marvels of the Canal 84

Chapter 19: How the Canal Helps Ships Save Time.................90

Chapter 20: The Future of the Panama Canal.......................96

Epilogue.. 102

Prologue

Imagine a journey where a ship has to sail thousands of extra miles just to get from one ocean to another. Before the Panama Canal was built, that's exactly what happened! Ships traveling from the east coast of the United States to the west coast had to go all the way around South America's southern tip—a dangerous and incredibly long voyage. But then, something amazing happened: engineers, leaders, and brave workers came together to carve a shortcut through the narrow land of Panama. This shortcut, known as the Panama Canal, changed the world forever.

The Panama Canal isn't just a waterway; it's one of the most impressive feats of engineering in human history. In this book, you'll discover how this incredible canal was built, the challenges that had to be overcome, and the many people who made it possible. You'll explore the unique design of the canal, its powerful locks, and learn why it remains one of the busiest and most important routes for ships today.

So, get ready to dive into the world of digging, designing, and daring adventures as we take a closer look at the story of the Panama Canal—an engineering marvel that's still making history!

Chapter 1: The Story Behind the Panama Canal

The story behind the Panama Canal is one of the most amazing tales of determination, human effort, and engineering in history. Imagine a huge shortcut that helps ships travel between two oceans without having to go all the way around the bottom of South America—that's what the Panama Canal does. But before it became the canal we know today, the journey to build it was full of challenges, dreams, and even some failures. It all began with the idea of making travel faster, because in the old days, ships had to make a long, dangerous trip around the tip of South America, called Cape Horn, which took a lot of time and was risky.

The story starts in the 1500s when explorers like Christopher Columbus and others were searching for new trade routes. People realized how helpful it would be to have a path through the narrow land in Central America, called the Isthmus of Panama, that could connect the Atlantic and Pacific Oceans. But back then, the technology didn't exist to create such a massive project. So, the dream of a canal remained just that—a dream—for many centuries. However, in the late 1800s, the idea of building a canal became more than just a dream. A French engineer named Ferdinand de Lesseps, who had already built the famous Suez Canal in Egypt, thought he could do the same in Panama. He believed it would be easy to dig a canal through the tropical rainforest. The French began working on it in 1881, and people were excited, thinking that soon ships would be able to sail from one ocean to the other. But things didn't go as planned.

The French effort quickly ran into trouble. The Panama region was incredibly difficult to work in because of the hot, humid weather, heavy rainfall, and thick jungle. But even worse than that were the diseases. Many workers became sick with malaria and yellow fever, which were spread by mosquitoes. Thousands of people died from these illnesses, and there were no good medicines or ways to stop the mosquitoes at the time. The French also underestimated how hard it would be to dig through the rocky, hilly land. Instead of the flat desert like in Egypt, Panama had mountains and rivers, and when it rained, the soil would turn to mud, making digging almost impossible. After several years of struggling, the French gave up in 1889, having spent a lot of money but making little progress. Their dream of building the Panama Canal had failed, leaving behind broken equipment and unfinished work.

Even though the French had failed, the idea of the canal didn't go away. The United States saw how important the canal could be for trade and military power. At the time, traveling around South America took too long, and a canal would save thousands of miles and many days for ships going from one coast to another. So, in the early 1900s, the United States decided to take over the project. But first, they needed permission from Panama, which was not yet its own country. At the time, Panama was part of Colombia, but the United States supported a movement that helped Panama become independent in 1903. In return, the new government of Panama agreed to let the U.S. build the canal.

Once the U.S. had control, they learned from the mistakes of the French. One of the first things they did was to get rid of the mosquitoes that were spreading diseases. Dr. William Gorgas, a doctor working in Panama, led the fight against malaria and yellow fever. He drained swamps, sprayed oil on water to stop mosquitoes from breeding, and used screens to protect workers from getting bitten. This helped save many lives and made it safer for people to work on the canal. Another big change the Americans made was how they planned to build the canal. Instead of trying to dig a sea-level canal like the French had tried, the Americans decided to build a system of locks. Locks are like huge water elevators that lift ships up and down so they can cross the canal even though the land is hilly. This idea of using locks made it possible to build the canal without digging through mountains, and it was a much better plan for the area.

The construction of the Panama Canal was still a huge challenge. Thousands of workers from all over the world, including many from the Caribbean islands, worked day and night to build it. They dug through dirt and rocks, blasted through hills with dynamite, and built the massive locks that would carry ships across the canal. One of the toughest parts of the job was digging through a place called the Culebra Cut, a deep valley that had to be carved out of the mountains. Landslides often slowed down progress, and heavy rains made it difficult to work, but the workers never gave up.

After more than ten years of hard work, the Panama Canal was finally completed in 1914. On August 15 of that year, the first ship, called the SS Ancon, sailed through the canal. It was a huge moment in history, and people around the world celebrated this incredible achievement. The canal was 50 miles long and included three sets of locks: one at the Pacific side, one at the Atlantic side, and one in the middle. These locks allowed ships to travel across the hilly land of Panama, rising and lowering them with water, like a giant staircase for boats. The Panama Canal became known as one of the greatest engineering marvels of all time.

The canal didn't just change travel; it changed the world. It made it much faster and easier for ships to move between the Atlantic and Pacific Oceans, which boosted trade and made global shipping more efficient. Instead of having to sail all the way around South America, ships could now cut through the canal in just a few hours. It also gave the United States more power in the region, as the canal was an important part of the country's military and economic strategy.

For many years, the Panama Canal was controlled by the United States, but in 1977, a treaty was signed to give control of the canal back to Panama. This transfer took place on December 31, 1999, and since then, Panama has been in charge of managing and operating the canal.

Over the years, the canal has been improved and expanded to handle bigger ships and more traffic, making it even more important in the world of global trade.

The story of the Panama Canal is not just about digging a big ditch through the jungle. It's a story about overcoming challenges, learning from mistakes, and working together to achieve something that seemed impossible. The canal continues to be a symbol of human ingenuity and determination, reminding us that with hard work and smart thinking, we can solve even the toughest problems. Today, the Panama Canal remains one of the most important waterways in the world, and every ship that passes through it carries with it the legacy of the people who made the dream of the canal a reality.

Chapter 2: How the Panama Canal Was Built

Building the Panama Canal was one of the most challenging and exciting engineering projects in history. It took a lot of planning, effort, and thousands of workers to turn the idea of connecting the Atlantic and Pacific Oceans into a reality. The Panama Canal was built through thick jungles, towering mountains, and mosquito-filled swamps, making it a true test of human strength and determination. The canal was built in the early 1900s, but the work that went into it started long before the first shovel hit the dirt. The process of building the canal is a fascinating story full of obstacles, triumphs, and amazing engineering solutions.

The first attempt to build the Panama Canal was made by the French in 1881. Ferdinand de Lesseps, the French engineer who had built the Suez Canal, thought he could do the same thing in Panama. The Suez Canal was built through the flat desert of Egypt, so Lesseps thought digging through the narrow strip of land in Panama wouldn't be too hard. He planned to create a sea-level canal, which meant digging a deep trench that connected both oceans, with no locks or special systems to help ships. However, Panama was very different from Egypt. The land was mountainous and covered in thick jungle, and the climate was hot, rainy, and full of mosquitoes that carried deadly diseases like malaria and yellow fever. This made working conditions terrible for the laborers.

The French quickly ran into problems. Thousands of workers got sick and died from diseases, and the equipment they brought couldn't handle the tough conditions. The land was also much harder to dig through than they expected. In the rainy season, the soil turned into sticky mud that made digging even harder, and the mountains were filled with rocks that were difficult to break apart. The French spent millions of dollars and many years trying to build the canal, but in 1889, they gave up, having made very little progress. The idea of a Panama Canal seemed impossible, and the jungle swallowed up their unfinished work.

But the dream of building a canal didn't die with the French. The United States saw how important a canal could be, both for trade and military power. In the early 1900s, the U.S. decided to take over the project. Before they could start building, they had to make a deal with Panama, which was part of Colombia at the time. After Panama gained its independence in 1903, the U.S. signed a treaty with the new country that allowed them to build the canal. With the legal issues settled, it was time to get to work.

One of the first challenges the Americans faced was dealing with the diseases that had killed so many French workers. Dr. William Gorgas, a doctor from the U.S. Army, led the effort to fight malaria and yellow fever. He realized that mosquitoes were spreading these diseases, so he and his team set out to get rid of the mosquitoes. They drained swamps where mosquitoes liked to breed, sprayed oil on standing water to kill mosquito eggs, and put screens on windows to keep mosquitoes out of buildings. Thanks to these efforts, the number of workers getting sick dropped dramatically, and it became much safer for people to work on the canal.

Another big change the Americans made was in their approach to building the canal. Instead of trying to create a sea-level canal like the French had, they decided to build a lock canal. A lock canal uses a series of huge chambers, called locks, to raise and lower ships as they travel through the canal. This meant they didn't have to dig as deep or cut through as much land, which made the project more realistic. The idea was to use water to lift ships up to the level of a man-made lake in the middle of the canal, and then lower them back down on the other side. These locks would be like giant water elevators, moving ships up and down as they crossed the isthmus.

Construction on the canal officially began in 1904. The first step was clearing the land and preparing the area for the massive work ahead. Workers had to remove trees, rocks, and other obstacles to create space for the canal and its locks. They also needed to build railroads to transport equipment and materials, like concrete, steel, and dynamite, which were used to dig through the mountains and build the locks. It was a huge task, and it required thousands of workers from around the world, including many from the Caribbean islands.

One of the toughest parts of building the canal was digging through a section known as the Culebra Cut, or Gaillard Cut. This was a nine-mile stretch through the mountains, and it required removing millions of cubic yards of earth and rock. The workers used dynamite to blast through the hardest sections, and steam shovels were brought in to dig out the rubble. However, the area was prone to landslides, especially during the rainy season, and this caused many setbacks. Each time there was a landslide, tons of dirt would come crashing down into the canal, filling in the areas that had already been dug out. Workers had to keep clearing it over and over again, which slowed down progress, but they never gave up.

At the same time, workers were busy building the enormous locks that would be needed to lift and lower ships. There were three sets of locks: one at Gatun, on the Atlantic side; one at Pedro Miguel; and another at Miraflores, on the Pacific side. Each lock chamber was huge, measuring over 1,000 feet long and wide enough to hold the largest ships of the time. The locks were made of concrete, and it took a massive amount of steel to build the gates that would open and close to let ships in and out. These gates were designed to be watertight and incredibly strong, as they had to hold back millions of gallons of water.

The locks worked by filling and draining water from the chambers using gravity. When a ship entered the first lock, the chamber would be filled with water, raising the ship to the next level. Then the gates would open, and the ship would move into the next chamber, where the process would be repeated. When the ship reached the highest point, it would sail through the man-made Gatun Lake, which had been created by damming the Chagres River. After crossing the lake, the ship would go through another series of locks, lowering it back down to sea level on the other side.

As the construction continued, the workers faced many other challenges, including intense heat, heavy rains, and dangerous working conditions. But they kept going, knowing that they were part of something that would change the world. The work was dangerous, and sadly, thousands of workers lost their lives during the project, many from accidents or diseases, despite the efforts to improve health conditions.

Finally, after ten years of hard work, the Panama Canal was completed. On August 15, 1914, the first ship, the SS Ancon, made its way through the canal, marking the beginning of a new era in global trade. The canal was 50 miles long and included the giant locks, the Culebra Cut, and Gatun Lake. It allowed ships to travel between the Atlantic and Pacific Oceans in just a few hours, saving them from the long and dangerous trip around the tip of South America.

The Panama Canal was an incredible achievement, not only because of the engineering skills it took to build but also because of the teamwork and dedication of the thousands of people who worked on it. The canal became one of the most important waterways in the world, helping to boost trade and making it easier for countries to connect with one another.

Over the years, the canal has been improved and expanded to handle larger ships and more traffic, but the basic design remains the same. Today, the Panama Canal is still considered one of the greatest engineering feats of all time, and it continues to be a vital part of global shipping. The story of how the Panama Canal was built is a reminder of what humans can achieve when they work together to overcome even the toughest challenges. The canal stands as a symbol of human ingenuity, hard work, and the desire to make the world a better, more connected place.

Chapter 3: Digging Through Mountains and Jungles

Digging through mountains and jungles to build the Panama Canal was one of the toughest parts of the entire project. Imagine trying to carve a path through towering, rocky mountains while surrounded by thick, humid jungles full of wild animals and insects. The landscape was not only difficult to navigate but also dangerous. The challenges of digging through such harsh terrain made this part of the construction a true test of strength, endurance, and engineering skill. The story of how workers and engineers tackled these natural obstacles is full of determination and ingenuity.

One of the biggest hurdles was a place called the Culebra Cut, also known as the Gaillard Cut. This section of the canal was nine miles long and sliced through the continental divide, a mountainous ridge that separated the Atlantic and Pacific watersheds. The Culebra Cut was filled with hard rock and dense soil, making it incredibly difficult to dig through. It was a central part of the canal's route, so there was no way around it. Workers had to dig down as much as 300 feet in some places to create a channel wide and deep enough for ships to pass through.

Digging through the Culebra Cut was a massive undertaking. Workers used dynamite to blast through the hardest rock. These explosions would break the rock into smaller pieces, which could then be hauled away. But dynamite was dangerous to use. Explosions had to be carefully controlled to prevent accidents. Workers would drill holes into the rock, place sticks of dynamite inside, and then retreat to a safe distance before setting off the charges. The blast would send rocks flying, and after the dust settled, teams of workers would move in with steam shovels and other equipment to clear the debris. However, even with all this effort, the work was slow, and there were frequent setbacks.

One of the biggest problems in the Culebra Cut was landslides. The mountains in this region were made of layers of rock and soil that were not very stable, especially when disturbed by digging. When it rained, the soil would become loose, and huge sections of the mountains would collapse into the canal. Sometimes, these landslides buried the work that had already been done, filling in areas that had taken months to dig out. Workers would have to start all over again, removing the same earth they had just cleared. Landslides caused constant delays, and they were dangerous too. Occasionally, workers were caught in the collapsing earth, and sadly, some lost their lives.

Despite the challenges, workers never gave up. They kept blasting, digging, and hauling away rock and dirt, slowly making progress. The engineers overseeing the project had to come up with clever solutions to deal with the landslides. One idea was to plant grass and other plants on the slopes of the mountains to help hold the soil together. They also designed the cut with sloping sides, instead of straight walls, to reduce the risk of landslides. These solutions helped, but the work remained dangerous and difficult.

While the mountains posed their own challenges, the jungles surrounding the canal were equally difficult to deal with. Panama is located in a tropical region, meaning the area around the canal was covered in dense, humid jungle filled with trees, vines, and thick undergrowth. Clearing this jungle was the first step in preparing the land for construction. Workers had to chop down trees, cut through vines, and remove stumps and roots from the ground. This was hard, exhausting work, especially in the sweltering heat and humidity of the Panama climate.

The jungle also brought other problems. The area was teeming with mosquitoes, many of which carried deadly diseases like malaria and yellow fever. Workers were constantly bitten by mosquitoes, and many became seriously ill. In fact, during the early stages of construction, more workers died from disease than from accidents or other causes.

The jungle was also home to dangerous animals, including snakes, and the thick vegetation made it difficult to see where you were stepping. On top of that, there were frequent heavy rains, which turned the ground into a muddy, slippery mess. Moving equipment and supplies through the jungle became incredibly challenging.

To make things easier, railroads were built to transport the materials needed for the canal's construction. Steam-powered trains would carry loads of dirt and rock away from the dig sites and bring in supplies like steel, concrete, and dynamite. Building these railroads through the jungle was a huge task in itself. Workers had to clear more land, lay down tracks, and keep the railroads running, even during the rainy season when the ground became waterlogged and unstable.

The weather was another major challenge for the workers. Panama experiences a rainy season that lasts for several months each year. During this time, the skies open up, and the rain falls in torrents. The ground would become so wet that it was nearly impossible to work. The rain also caused rivers and streams to swell, often flooding the work sites and washing away equipment. Workers had to wait for the rain to stop before they could continue, and sometimes entire weeks were lost to bad weather. The constant downpours made it difficult to maintain a steady pace, but the workers pressed on, determined to complete the project.

One of the most important parts of building the canal was creating the massive artificial lake known as Gatun Lake. To do this, workers had to dam the Chagres River, one of the largest rivers in Panama. The Chagres River flowed through the jungle and often caused flooding, which made it a challenge for the construction teams. By building a dam, engineers were able to control the flow of the river and create a large, calm body of water that ships could pass through. The dam itself was a huge structure made of concrete and earth, and building it required thousands of workers and tons of material.

Once the dam was completed, the area behind it began to fill with water, forming Gatun Lake. The lake was an important part of the canal because it allowed ships to travel across the highest point of the isthmus without needing to dig a continuous sea-level channel. The lake also acted as a reservoir, storing water that was used to operate the canal's locks. The construction of Gatun Lake transformed the landscape, flooding what had once been dense jungle and creating a calm waterway that would be a key part of the canal's success.

Another key feature of the canal was the locks. The locks allowed ships to be raised up to the level of Gatun Lake and then lowered back down to sea level on the other side. Building the locks was a huge engineering challenge. Each lock chamber was over 1,000 feet long and as tall as an eight-story building. The walls of the locks were made of thick concrete, and the gates were constructed from heavy steel. These gates had to be strong enough to hold back the millions of gallons of water that would fill the locks. Workers used cranes and other heavy equipment to lift the steel gates into place, and the process required extreme precision.

The locks were powered by gravity, which meant that no pumps were needed to move water in and out of the chambers. Instead, engineers designed a system of culverts and valves that allowed water to flow from the lake into the locks. When a ship entered the first lock chamber, water would be released, filling the chamber and raising the ship to the next level. The gates would then open, allowing the ship to move forward to the next chamber. This process was repeated until the ship reached Gatun Lake, where it could sail across before going through another set of locks on the other side. This system made it possible for even the largest ships to pass through the canal.

The entire project of digging through mountains and jungles took years to complete. It required thousands of workers, tons of equipment, and a great deal of perseverance. Many workers faced difficult and dangerous conditions, but their hard work paid off in the end. By the time the canal was finished in 1914, it was considered one of the greatest engineering achievements of all time. The Panama Canal not only connected two oceans, but it also symbolized human determination and the ability to overcome even the toughest obstacles.

Today, the Panama Canal is still an essential part of global trade, with ships from all over the world passing through it every day. The story of how the canal was built, from digging through mountains and jungles to constructing the massive locks and dams, is a testament to the ingenuity and courage of the people who worked on it. Despite the difficulties they faced, they never gave up, and their efforts changed the world forever.

Chapter 4: The Incredible Locks of the Panama Canal

The locks of the Panama Canal are truly one of the most incredible features of this engineering marvel. They are like giant water elevators that lift massive ships up and over the rugged terrain of Panama, then lower them back down to sea level on the other side. Without these locks, it would have been impossible to build the canal because digging a completely flat, sea-level channel through the mountainous landscape would have been far too difficult and expensive. The locks are a brilliant solution that make it possible for ships to cross from the Atlantic Ocean to the Pacific Ocean (and vice versa) without having to sail all the way around South America.

There are three sets of locks on the Panama Canal: one set on the Atlantic side at Gatun, and two on the Pacific side at Pedro Miguel and Miraflores. Each lock system is made up of large chambers where ships enter and are raised or lowered by the water level. The basic idea behind the locks is simple: water flows into the chambers to raise ships or drains out to lower them. But while the concept may be easy to understand, the actual construction and operation of the locks is a masterpiece of engineering.

The locks work by taking advantage of gravity and water pressure. When a ship approaches the Panama Canal, it first enters one of the lock chambers. These chambers are massive — over 1,000 feet long and 110 feet wide — and they're built out of thick concrete to withstand the immense pressure of the water they hold. Once the ship is inside, giant steel gates close behind it. These gates are as tall as an eight-story building and weigh hundreds of tons, yet they can be opened and closed with the precision of a well-oiled machine.

Once the gates are closed, water from the artificial Gatun Lake is allowed to flow into the chamber through a system of underground culverts. The water enters the chamber beneath the ship, gently lifting it as the water level rises. This process is done using gravity, which means that no pumps are required to move the water — it simply flows from the higher level of the lake into the lower level of the lock chamber. As the chamber fills with water, the ship is slowly raised, sometimes by as much as 85 feet. It's a slow but steady process, taking about 10 minutes to raise a ship fully.

When the ship has been raised to the right level, the gates in front of it open, allowing the ship to move into the next chamber, where the process is repeated. This continues until the ship reaches the highest point of the canal, which is the level of Gatun Lake. After crossing the lake, the ship enters another set of locks on the opposite side, where the process is reversed, and the ship is lowered back down to sea level. On its journey through the canal, a ship is raised and lowered a total of about 170 feet.

One of the most remarkable things about the locks is how smoothly they operate. The entire system is controlled by a team of lock operators who oversee every step of the process. Even though the ships passing through the canal are enormous — some of them are longer than the locks themselves — they move through the system with incredible precision. Tugboats help guide the ships into position, and a set of electric locomotives called "mules" are used to pull the ships through the locks. These mules are attached to the ships with thick cables and keep them centered in the lock chamber to prevent them from bumping into the walls. Each lock chamber is just wide enough to accommodate the largest ships, with only a few feet of space on either side, so careful control is essential.

The locks are designed to handle ships of all sizes, but they were originally built to accommodate the largest ships of the early 20th century, known as "Panamax" vessels. Panamax ships are specifically sized to fit within the locks, with a maximum length of 965 feet and a width of 106 feet. However, as ships have grown larger over the years, a new set of locks called the "Panama Canal Expansion" or "Third Set of Locks" was opened in 2016. These new locks are even bigger, allowing a new class of ships known as "New Panamax" or "Post-Panamax" vessels to pass through. These ships can carry far more cargo than their predecessors, making the canal even more valuable for global trade.

The construction of the locks was one of the most challenging parts of building the Panama Canal. Each lock chamber had to be large enough to hold not only the ships but also millions of gallons of water. The walls of the locks are made from reinforced concrete, and in some places, they are more than 50 feet thick. This is because the locks have to withstand the enormous pressure exerted by the water they hold. The gates, which are made of steel, are designed to be watertight, so no water leaks between the chambers. Even though the gates are incredibly heavy, they float on special bearings, which makes them easier to move.

One of the most ingenious aspects of the lock system is how water is reused. Instead of allowing the water to simply flow out into the ocean after each ship passes through, the water is carefully controlled and directed back into the lake or into other lock chambers. This recycling of water helps conserve one of the canal's most precious resources. Without this system, it would take far more water to operate the locks, and the canal might run out of water during the dry season.

The locks are also designed to be incredibly reliable. Even though they were built over 100 years ago, the original locks still operate much the same way they did when the canal first opened in 1914. Over the years, the lock system has been maintained and upgraded to ensure that it continues to function smoothly. This includes replacing old equipment with newer technology, such as installing electric motors to operate the gates and improving the control systems used by the lock operators.

One of the most fascinating things about the locks is how they are operated. In the early days, the entire system was controlled manually, with lock operators using levers and switches to control the flow of water and the movement of the gates. Today, much of the process is automated, but human operators still play a critical role. From a control tower overlooking the locks, the operators monitor the movement of ships, adjust the water levels, and ensure that everything is running smoothly. It's a job that requires great attention to detail because even a small mistake could cause delays or accidents.

The locks of the Panama Canal are not only a feat of engineering but also a vital part of the world's shipping network. Every day, dozens of ships pass through the canal, carrying goods like cars, oil, food, and machinery. The canal has dramatically shortened the time it takes for ships to travel between the Atlantic and Pacific oceans, making global trade faster and more efficient. Without the locks, ships would have to sail all the way around the southern tip of South America, adding thousands of miles and weeks to their journeys.

Despite being over a century old, the locks of the Panama Canal remain a marvel of modern engineering. They are a testament to human ingenuity and determination, showing that with the right tools and ideas, we can overcome even the most daunting challenges. The locks are also a reminder of how much hard work and effort went into building the canal. Thousands of workers from all over the world came to Panama to help build the locks, and their legacy lives on in the smooth operation of the canal today.

As the world continues to change, the Panama Canal and its incredible locks will remain an essential part of global trade. With the addition of the new, larger locks, the canal is ready to handle the next generation of ships, ensuring that it will continue to be a vital link between the oceans for many years to come. The story of the locks is not just about water and steel; it's about vision, perseverance, and the ability to turn a dream into reality.

Chapter 5: Meet Ferdinand de Lesseps: The Canal Dreamer

Ferdinand de Lesseps was a man with a grand vision, and that vision was to connect two oceans by digging a canal through Panama. He was a dreamer who believed that it was possible to create a shortcut that would allow ships to avoid the long and dangerous journey around the southern tip of South America. His name is most famously associated with the Suez Canal, a massive project that successfully connected the Mediterranean Sea to the Red Sea, but his dream of building the Panama Canal was even bigger. Though things didn't go as planned, Ferdinand de Lesseps' story is one of ambition, determination, and the pursuit of a nearly impossible goal.

Born in France in 1805, Ferdinand de Lesseps came from a family that had strong ties to diplomacy and engineering. His father was a diplomat, and young Ferdinand followed in his footsteps by entering the diplomatic service when he was still a young man. He traveled to many different countries, representing France and learning about the world. But it was during his time in Egypt that he became fascinated by the idea of building canals. Egypt was a land of deserts and ancient pyramids, and it had long been a place where people dreamed of connecting bodies of water to make trade and travel easier. That's where de Lesseps first heard about plans to dig a canal that would link the Mediterranean Sea with the Red Sea.

At that time, many people thought such a project was impossible. The Suez region was dry, and digging a canal through the desert seemed like a crazy idea. But de Lesseps was not one to be discouraged by such challenges. He was a man who believed that with enough hard work, vision, and cooperation, anything could be achieved. So, he gathered support from leaders and engineers, and in 1859, construction on the Suez Canal began. It was a huge undertaking, requiring thousands of workers and years of effort, but de Lesseps stayed focused on his dream. In 1869, the Suez Canal was completed, and Ferdinand de Lesseps was celebrated as a hero. The canal dramatically shortened the journey between Europe and Asia, transforming global trade.

After the success of the Suez Canal, de Lesseps set his sights on an even more ambitious project: the Panama Canal. He believed that if he could connect the Atlantic and Pacific Oceans, it would be one of the greatest achievements in human history. The idea of a canal through Central America was not new—people had been dreaming about it for centuries. But the challenges of digging through the mountainous, jungle-covered terrain of Panama were far greater than the challenges of the flat, sandy desert around Suez.

In 1879, de Lesseps traveled to Panama to explore the possibility of building the canal. He was confident that he could replicate the success he had achieved in Egypt, and he quickly gathered a team of investors, engineers, and workers. In his speeches and presentations, he spoke of the canal as a project that would unite the world by bringing people and goods closer together. He called it a "civilizing mission" and said that the canal would bring prosperity to Panama and all the countries that traded through it.

But Panama was not like Egypt. While the Suez Canal had been built in a relatively dry, open area, the Panama region was covered in thick jungle and home to many dangerous animals, diseases, and unpredictable weather patterns. The tropical climate brought with it constant rain and unbearable heat, and the dense vegetation made construction extremely difficult. On top of that, there was the problem of the mountains. While Suez was flat, Panama had towering peaks that would have to be carved away to create a path for the canal. Ferdinand de Lesseps, however, remained undeterred. He believed that his experience with the Suez Canal had prepared him for the challenges ahead, and he was convinced that the Panama Canal could be completed using similar methods.

Construction began in 1881, but almost immediately, the project ran into trouble. The terrain was far more difficult to dig through than anyone had expected. Instead of sand and rock, the workers encountered thick clay and muddy soil that constantly collapsed, filling in the trenches they had dug. The dense jungle also harbored mosquitoes, which carried deadly diseases like malaria and yellow fever. Thousands of workers became ill, and many died. Despite these setbacks, de Lesseps refused to give up. He was a man who had always believed in the power of perseverance, and he continued to push forward, convinced that success was just around the corner.

One of the major challenges that de Lesseps and his team faced was figuring out how to deal with the Chagres River, a powerful river that flowed through the middle of the canal route. During the rainy season, the river would swell and flood the construction site, washing away months of hard work. De Lesseps' original plan was to build the canal at sea level, just like the Suez Canal, which meant that the river would have to be diverted or controlled in some way. But no matter how hard the engineers tried, they couldn't find a way to tame the Chagres River. The constant flooding made construction nearly impossible, and the cost of the project skyrocketed.

Despite these mounting difficulties, de Lesseps remained optimistic. He continued to raise money for the project and gave speeches about how important the canal would be for the future of global trade. But as the years went on, it became clear that the project was in serious trouble. The sea-level plan simply wasn't going to work in Panama, and the number of worker deaths from disease and accidents kept rising. By 1888, the French Panama Canal project was bankrupt, and work on the canal ground to a halt. It was a devastating blow for Ferdinand de Lesseps, who had poured his heart and soul into the project.

In the end, the French effort to build the Panama Canal was a failure, and de Lesseps' dream of connecting the Atlantic and Pacific

Oceans seemed to be over. He was deeply disappointed, and the collapse of the project tarnished his reputation. He had gone from being hailed as a hero for the Suez Canal to being criticized for the disaster in Panama. But despite the failure, de Lesseps' vision lived on. His dream of a canal through Panama had inspired many people, and although it would take years, others would eventually pick up where he had left off.

Ferdinand de Lesseps didn't live to see the completion of the Panama Canal, which was finally finished by the United States in 1914. But his contribution to the canal's story is undeniable. He was the first to truly believe that a canal through Panama could be built, and although he didn't succeed, his determination and belief in the project helped lay the groundwork for the future. The Panama Canal is, in many ways, a tribute to dreamers like Ferdinand de Lesseps who dared to imagine the impossible.

Today, the Panama Canal is one of the most important waterways in the world, and it continues to play a vital role in global trade. While de Lesseps' vision of a sea-level canal didn't come to pass, the modern canal uses locks to raise and lower ships as they pass through the mountains and jungles of Panama. It's an engineering wonder that has changed the way the world works, and it all began with the dreams of a man named Ferdinand de Lesseps. His story reminds us that even though not all dreams come true, the act of dreaming can inspire great things.

Chapter 6: How Ships Travel Through the Canal

Imagine you're the captain of a huge ship sailing from the Atlantic Ocean, and you're about to embark on a journey through one of the greatest engineering marvels in the world, the Panama Canal. This incredible waterway is like a giant shortcut between the Atlantic and Pacific Oceans, saving ships thousands of miles of travel. But getting through the canal isn't as simple as just sailing straight across from one side to the other. There's a whole process involved, and it's pretty amazing how it all works. Let's take a closer look at how ships travel through the Panama Canal and what happens at each step of the way.

First, when a ship arrives at the entrance of the Panama Canal, it must wait its turn. The canal is a busy place, with hundreds of ships passing through each week, so there's often a bit of a wait before a ship can enter. Ships line up in the nearby waters, sometimes forming what looks like a giant parking lot of boats floating on the ocean. While waiting, the ship's captain and crew prepare for the journey ahead. They know they'll need to navigate through narrow passages, huge locks, and areas that are controlled by powerful machines.

Once it's the ship's turn to enter the canal, a special team of people comes aboard to help. These people are called canal pilots, and they are experts in guiding ships through the Panama Canal. Even though the ship's captain is experienced, the canal pilots know every twist, turn, and challenge of the canal, so they take control of the ship for the journey. Their job is incredibly important because the Panama Canal is not like the open ocean—it's a complex system of waterways, locks, and lakes, and only skilled pilots who know the canal inside and out can safely navigate it.

The first major part of the journey is entering the system of locks that will lift the ship up to the level of Gatun Lake, which sits about

85 feet (26 meters) above sea level. The locks are like giant elevators for ships, and they're one of the most fascinating parts of the canal. When the ship reaches the first lock, it's slowly guided into a massive chamber made of thick concrete. These chambers are so large that they can fit ships the size of skyscrapers lying on their side! Once the ship is inside the lock, huge gates close behind it, sealing the chamber. These gates are super strong and weigh as much as several elephants, but they open and close smoothly thanks to the engineering brilliance of the canal's designers.

With the ship safely inside the lock, the real magic begins. Water starts to fill the chamber, and as the water level rises, the ship rises with it. It's an incredible sight to see a massive ship being lifted by nothing more than water. The water that fills the lock comes from nearby Gatun Lake, and it flows into the chamber through special tunnels built beneath the lock. It takes only a few minutes for the chamber to fill with millions of gallons of water, and by the time it's full, the ship has been lifted up to the next level.

This process is repeated as the ship moves through the different locks, rising higher and higher until it reaches the level of Gatun Lake. Each time the ship enters a new lock, it's guided in by electric locomotives called "mules." These mules don't pull the ship like traditional animals pulling carts; instead, they run on tracks alongside the locks and use cables to keep the ship steady and in place as it moves forward. Without the mules, the ship could drift or bump into the walls of the locks, which could cause serious damage to both the ship and the canal. The mules ensure that everything runs smoothly and safely.

After the ship has been raised up to the level of Gatun Lake, it enters the next stage of the journey: crossing the lake itself. Gatun Lake is a huge man-made lake that was created when the Chagres River was dammed during the construction of the canal. It's an important part of the Panama Canal system because it provides the water needed to fill the locks and allows ships to travel a large portion of the canal without needing more locks. Sailing across Gatun Lake can take several hours, depending on the size and speed of the ship. The lake is surrounded by lush rainforests, and if you're lucky, you might spot wildlife like birds or even monkeys as you pass through this tropical paradise.

After crossing Gatun Lake, the ship reaches the narrowest and most challenging part of the Panama Canal: the Culebra Cut. This section was carved through the mountains, and it's a winding, narrow channel that requires precise navigation. The canal pilots are especially careful here because the Culebra Cut is not only tight, but it also has steep walls that could cause trouble if a ship were to drift too far off course. As the ship makes its way through the cut, it's a tense and exciting part of the journey. There's not much room for error, but thanks to the skill of the canal pilots and the ship's crew, most ships make it through safely.

Once the ship has passed through the Culebra Cut, it's time for the final part of the journey: descending back down to sea level on the other side. Just like on the Atlantic side of the canal, there are a series of locks on the Pacific side that lower ships down. But instead of filling the locks with water to lift the ship, this time the water is drained out, and the ship slowly sinks as the water level drops. It's the opposite of what happened earlier in the journey, but it's just as impressive. Each time the ship enters a new lock, the water is carefully drained out, and the ship is lowered by about 28 feet (8.5 meters) until it reaches sea level.

As the ship passes through the final lock and out into the Pacific Ocean, the journey through the Panama Canal is complete. What took days or even weeks of sailing around the southern tip of South America now takes only about 8 to 10 hours through the canal. The ship has been lifted up and then lowered back down, guided through mountains and jungles, and helped by machines, water, and people working together. It's an extraordinary example of human engineering and the power of cooperation to make something incredible happen.

One of the most amazing things about the Panama Canal is how efficient it is. Despite being built over 100 years ago, the canal still operates with remarkable precision, handling some of the biggest ships in the world every single day. The locks are still controlled by many of the same systems that were in place when the canal first opened, and they continue to work flawlessly. While new technology has been added over the years, the basic design of the canal remains the same, and it's a testament to the brilliance of the engineers who created it.

Ships from all over the world rely on the Panama Canal to transport goods between the Atlantic and Pacific Oceans. Whether it's containers filled with electronics, food, cars, or clothing, the canal plays a crucial role in the global economy. The shortcut it provides saves time, fuel, and money, making it one of the most important waterways on the planet. Without it, shipping would be slower and more expensive, and many of the things we use every day might take much longer to reach us.

As the ship sails away from the Panama Canal and out into the Pacific Ocean, it's hard not to feel a sense of awe at what has just happened. The ship has traveled through one of the greatest shortcuts in history, thanks to the incredible locks, the canal pilots, and the engineering brilliance that made it all possible. The Panama Canal truly is a wonder of the modern world, and the journey through it is an unforgettable experience.

Chapter 7: The Challenges of Building the Canal

Building the Panama Canal was one of the most challenging engineering projects ever undertaken. Imagine trying to cut a pathway for ships through thick jungles, towering mountains, and a land teeming with dangerous animals, all while dealing with extreme weather and deadly diseases. The people who worked on the canal faced nearly every obstacle you could think of, and it took decades of effort, multiple failed attempts, and a lot of courage to finally complete the waterway that connected the Atlantic and Pacific Oceans. Let's dive into the incredible story of the challenges of building the Panama Canal.

The story of the Panama Canal begins long before the first shovel of dirt was moved. For centuries, people dreamed of finding a way to connect the two oceans, making trade and travel much easier and faster. But the biggest problem was geography. The narrow strip of land that is Panama is not flat—it's a rugged, mountainous region covered in dense rainforests, with rivers, swamps, and wetlands that make travel extremely difficult. This wasn't going to be an easy place to build anything, let alone a massive canal that could handle the largest ships in the world.

The first serious attempt to build the canal came in the late 1800s, led by a Frenchman named Ferdinand de Lesseps. He was famous for his success in building the Suez Canal in Egypt, which had connected the Mediterranean Sea to the Red Sea and was seen as one of the greatest engineering achievements of the time. Confident from his success, de Lesseps believed that building the Panama Canal would be just as easy. He was wrong. While the Suez Canal was built through flat desert land, Panama was an entirely different challenge. The thick, humid jungles were full of snakes, insects, and other creatures that made life difficult for workers. The mountainous terrain meant that instead of digging a straightforward channel, workers would have to cut through hills and valleys. On top of that, the tropical climate brought heavy rains and intense heat, making the work grueling and dangerous.

One of the biggest challenges was disease. Panama was a hotbed for two of the deadliest diseases in the world at the time: malaria and yellow fever. These diseases were spread by mosquitoes, and in the 19th century, no one really knew how to stop them. Workers would arrive in Panama full of hope and energy, ready to take on the challenge of building the canal, but many would fall sick within days or weeks. Yellow fever caused high fevers, severe pain, and often death, while malaria caused chills, fever, and weakness that could last for months. Hospitals quickly filled up with sick workers, and doctors had no way to treat these illnesses. Many workers died, and others were too weak to continue working. It became clear that disease was going to be one of the biggest obstacles to building the canal.

Another major challenge was the terrain itself. The land was not just hilly—it was full of rivers and swamps that made it nearly impossible to bring in machinery or supplies. Workers had to dig through mud that seemed to swallow up their tools and equipment. And then there was the Culebra Cut, the most difficult section of the canal to dig. This was a deep, narrow valley that needed to be cut through the mountains. It was a massive excavation project, and workers had to dig through solid rock and dirt. Landslides were common, with tons of earth and rock suddenly collapsing into the canal, burying equipment and sometimes even workers. The sheer scale of the digging was overwhelming, and progress was slow. Dealing with these constant landslides was like trying to empty a bathtub while the faucet was still running.

The weather also played a major role in the difficulties faced by the workers. Panama has a tropical climate, with a rainy season that lasts for months. During this time, torrential downpours would flood the work sites, turning the ground into a swampy mess. The rains made it difficult to dig, and the mud would often trap machinery, slowing progress even further. Workers would arrive in the morning only to find their previous day's work completely undone by the night's rain. And when it wasn't raining, the heat was stifling. Workers had to deal with temperatures that often soared above 100 degrees Fahrenheit (38 degrees Celsius), and the humidity made the air feel even heavier. The heat exhausted the workers, many of whom were already weakened by disease and poor living conditions.

The French effort to build the canal ultimately failed. After years of hard work, disease, and landslides, the project ran out of money, and the French had to abandon their dream of building the canal. Thousands of workers had died, and the canal was left unfinished, with only a fraction of the digging complete. It seemed like the dream of a Panama Canal might never be realized.

But in the early 20th century, the United States decided to take on the challenge. Under the leadership of President Theodore Roosevelt, the U.S. bought the rights to continue the canal project from the French and began the massive task of finishing what had been started. The Americans knew that they couldn't succeed where the French had failed unless they tackled the problems of disease and terrain head-on.

The first thing they did was focus on eradicating the mosquitoes that spread malaria and yellow fever. A man named Dr. William Gorgas was put in charge of cleaning up Panama. He organized a huge campaign to drain swamps, clear standing water, and fumigate buildings to kill mosquitoes. Workers set up mosquito nets and wore protective clothing to avoid getting bitten. Thanks to Gorgas's efforts, the number of cases of malaria and yellow fever dropped dramatically, and workers were able to stay healthy enough to continue building the canal. This was a major breakthrough and allowed work to proceed at a much faster pace than before.

The Americans also tackled the engineering challenges of the canal in a new way. Instead of trying to dig a sea-level canal like the French had attempted, the U.S. engineers decided to build a canal with locks. These locks would lift ships up to the level of a man-made lake in the middle of Panama, allowing ships to cross the highlands without having to dig all the way through the mountains. This new approach made the project much more manageable, but it still required an enormous amount of work.

The Culebra Cut, the most difficult part of the canal, continued to cause problems for the Americans just as it had for the French. Landslides remained a constant threat, and workers had to dig through rock and dirt while being careful to avoid dangerous collapses. Dynamite was used to blast through the hardest rock, and massive steam shovels, some of the largest machines in the world at the time, were brought in to move the earth. It was backbreaking work, and many workers were injured or killed in accidents. But slowly, bit by bit, the canal began to take shape.

The Panama Canal also required the construction of huge dams to create the man-made lakes that would supply water to the locks. The Gatun Dam, in particular, was a massive undertaking. It created Gatun Lake, which would serve as a key part of the canal, providing the water needed to lift and lower ships as they passed through the locks. Building the dam involved moving tons of earth and rock, and it took years to complete. But once it was finished, it allowed the canal to operate smoothly, with ships being able to travel across the lake instead of having to navigate more locks.

The work on the Panama Canal took more than a decade, and the challenges never really stopped. From the deadly diseases that claimed the lives of thousands of workers to the constant threat of landslides and the sheer difficulty of moving earth and rock, the project was filled with obstacles. But in 1914, the Panama Canal was finally completed. Ships could now travel between the Atlantic and Pacific Oceans in just a few hours, instead of taking the long and dangerous journey around the southern tip of South America.

The completion of the Panama Canal was a triumph of human ingenuity and determination. It showed that with the right combination of technology, hard work, and perseverance, even the most daunting challenges could be overcome. The workers who built the canal faced incredible hardships, but they never gave up. Their efforts created one of the most important waterways in the world, a canal that continues to be a vital part of global trade to this day. The Panama Canal stands as a reminder of what people can accomplish when they work together to tackle even the toughest problems.

Chapter 8: The Role of Teddy Roosevelt in the Panama Canal

The story of the Panama Canal is not just about digging through mountains and jungles; it's also a tale of bold leadership and vision. One of the most important figures in the creation of the Panama Canal was none other than Theodore "Teddy" Roosevelt, the 26th president of the United States. Roosevelt's role in the canal's construction was essential, as he pushed for its completion, guided decisions, and took some bold actions that changed the course of history. Without him, the Panama Canal might never have been completed, or at least not in the way it eventually came to be. His involvement wasn't just about engineering but about politics, diplomacy, and sheer determination.

When Roosevelt became president in 1901, the idea of a canal connecting the Atlantic and Pacific Oceans had been around for centuries. People had long dreamed of a way to shorten the long and dangerous voyage ships had to take around the southern tip of South America. The French had already attempted to build a canal through Panama in the 1880s, led by Ferdinand de Lesseps, who had successfully overseen the construction of the Suez Canal. But that project had ended in failure due to disease, financial problems, and the overwhelming difficulty of the terrain. By the time Roosevelt became president, the French had left behind an unfinished project and a lot of abandoned equipment.

Roosevelt recognized how important the canal would be for the United States and the world. He saw it as a way to boost trade, increase military strength, and cement the U.S. as a global power. A canal through Panama would allow American ships, both commercial and military, to move between the Atlantic and Pacific Oceans much faster. This was especially important for the U.S. Navy, as it meant ships could quickly be sent to defend American interests in either ocean without having to sail all the way around South America. Roosevelt was determined to make the canal a reality, and he was willing to take bold steps to get it done.

One of the first obstacles Roosevelt faced was political. Panama was not yet an independent country; it was part of Colombia. The U.S. had initially tried to negotiate with Colombia to gain control over the land needed to build the canal. A treaty was proposed that would allow the U.S. to lease a strip of land across Panama in exchange for money, but the Colombian government rejected the deal. This was a major setback, but Roosevelt wasn't about to give up. He believed that the canal was too important to let political obstacles stand in the way.

Here's where Roosevelt's bold and controversial leadership came into play. Around the same time as the negotiations with Colombia were falling apart, there was a growing movement in Panama for independence. Many Panamanians were unhappy with Colombian rule and wanted to break away to form their own country. Roosevelt saw an opportunity and decided to support the Panamanian independence movement. He quietly encouraged Panamanian rebels to declare their independence from Colombia, and in 1903, they did just that. The U.S. Navy was stationed nearby to ensure that Colombian forces couldn't easily suppress the rebellion. Within days, the U.S. recognized the new nation of Panama, and shortly afterward, Panama agreed to let the United States build the canal. This move was highly controversial. Some people accused Roosevelt of using underhanded tactics to get what he wanted, but Roosevelt believed that the ends justified the means.

With the political roadblocks out of the way, Roosevelt turned his attention to the actual construction of the canal. He was deeply involved in the project and was determined to see it succeed where the French had failed. One of the first things he did was appoint a team of experienced engineers and leaders to oversee the work. Roosevelt knew that the task ahead was enormous, but he had confidence that with the right people in charge, the canal could be completed.

Roosevelt also understood that the health problems that had plagued the French effort would need to be addressed before any real progress could be made. Panama was full of mosquitoes that spread deadly diseases like malaria and yellow fever. Thousands of workers had died during the French attempt to build the canal, and Roosevelt knew that unless these diseases were brought under control, the U.S. effort would face the same fate. Roosevelt supported a major public health campaign, led by Dr. William Gorgas, to eradicate mosquitoes in the canal zone. Gorgas organized teams to drain swamps, clear out standing water, and fumigate homes and work areas. These efforts dramatically reduced the number of cases of malaria and yellow fever, allowing workers to stay healthy and continue working. Without this focus on public health, it's likely that the U.S. would have faced the same disastrous problems as the French.

Another challenge Roosevelt had to deal with was the engineering of the canal itself. The French had attempted to build a sea-level canal, meaning that ships would have sailed through without having to be lifted or lowered. But this approach proved to be too difficult due to the mountainous terrain in Panama. Roosevelt's engineers decided to take a different approach: they would build a canal with locks. Locks are like water elevators that raise and lower ships to different levels as they move through the canal. This new design was more practical and allowed the canal to pass through the mountains without having to dig all the way down to sea level. Roosevelt supported this plan, knowing that it would make the project more feasible, even though it required a lot of additional work to build the locks and the giant man-made lakes that would supply them with water.

One of Roosevelt's most famous moments during the construction of the canal was when he visited the site in 1906. This was the first time a sitting U.S. president had ever traveled outside the country while in office, and it showed just how personally invested Roosevelt was in the project. He toured the construction site, met with workers, and even took a turn at operating one of the giant steam shovels that was being used to dig the canal. Photos of Roosevelt sitting at the controls of the steam shovel were widely circulated, and they helped solidify his image as a hands-on leader who wasn't afraid to get involved in the hard work. His visit also boosted the morale of the workers, who were inspired by the president's enthusiasm and commitment to the project.

Roosevelt's role in the Panama Canal wasn't just about overseeing the construction. He also had to deal with critics back home who questioned whether the canal was worth the cost and effort. Building the canal was incredibly expensive, and it took years of hard, dangerous work to make progress. Some people thought that the money could be better spent elsewhere, or that the U.S. shouldn't be involved in such a risky foreign project. But Roosevelt believed that the canal was essential for the future of the United States. He argued that it would open up new opportunities for trade, strengthen the military, and help the U.S. play a bigger role in world affairs. Roosevelt was known for his philosophy of "big stick" diplomacy—meaning that the U.S. should negotiate peacefully but also be ready to use its power when necessary. He saw the Panama Canal as a key part of that vision, as it would give the U.S. Navy the ability to quickly move ships between the two oceans, ensuring that the country could defend its interests around the world.

By the time the Panama Canal was completed in 1914, Roosevelt was no longer president, but his influence on the project was undeniable. He had been the driving force behind the canal's construction, pushing through political obstacles, supporting public health efforts, and backing the engineering decisions that made the canal a success. Roosevelt often said that he considered the Panama Canal one of his greatest achievements, and he was right to feel proud. The canal transformed global trade and helped establish the United

States as a major world power. It also showed the world what could be accomplished with determination, innovation, and strong leadership.

Teddy Roosevelt's role in the Panama Canal was about more than just a construction project. It was about vision, leadership, and a belief in the power of the United States to shape its own future. Roosevelt didn't just want to build a canal—he wanted to build a symbol of American strength and ingenuity. And that's exactly what the Panama Canal became. It remains one of the greatest engineering achievements in history, and it's a lasting testament to Roosevelt's bold and determined leadership. Without his determination and vision, the Panama Canal might still be a dream, rather than the reality it is today.

Chapter 9: Life in the Panama Canal Zone

The Panama Canal Zone was a unique place, unlike anywhere else in the world. It was a strip of land about 10 miles wide that stretched across Panama, where the Panama Canal was built. While most people think of the canal as an incredible engineering marvel, what many don't realize is that the zone itself was almost like its own little world, with its own way of life. For the people who lived and worked there, life in the Panama Canal Zone was an adventure, filled with hard work, different cultures, and a mix of challenges and rewards.

Life in the Panama Canal Zone started with the workers, both American and local, who came from all over the world to build and operate the canal. Many of these workers were from the United States, but there were also people from the Caribbean islands, Europe, and other parts of Latin America. The American workers usually held higher-ranking jobs, like engineers, doctors, and managers, while many of the laborers and lower-ranking workers were from the Caribbean or Panama itself. This created a community that was very diverse, but also divided in many ways.

The canal zone had a unique structure. It was under the control of the United States, even though it was located in Panama. This meant that the laws, services, and schools were all American, and people living in the zone followed U.S. rules. It felt almost like a little piece of America planted right in the middle of Panama. American families lived in neat, organized neighborhoods with schools, hospitals, and stores that were just like those in the U.S. They even used American money, spoke English, and celebrated American holidays. In some ways, it was like a small town that had been picked up from the U.S. and moved to Central America.

For the Americans who lived in the zone, life was comfortable, but it also came with a sense of isolation. Many of the workers lived in government housing, which was built specifically for them. These houses were often well-constructed and provided a high standard of living compared to the homes outside the zone. The American families in the zone enjoyed modern conveniences, like electricity, running water, and even air conditioning, which made living in the hot, humid climate much more bearable. There were schools for the children, where they learned the same subjects as kids in the U.S., and there were hospitals that offered medical care to the workers and their families.

The Panama Canal Zone was very different from the surrounding areas in Panama, and this created a feeling of separation. American workers had their own schools, clubs, and entertainment, and they mostly socialized with other Americans. There were theaters where American movies were shown, sports clubs where baseball and basketball were played, and social gatherings like picnics and dances. The people in the zone had a close-knit community, but it could feel like they were cut off from the rest of Panama. Many American families rarely ventured outside the canal zone, and when they did, they sometimes felt like they were in a foreign country, even though they were just a short distance away.

For the local workers from Panama and the Caribbean, life in the canal zone was different. They often lived in separate areas from the American workers and had different facilities. These areas were usually not as modern or well-kept as the American neighborhoods. Local workers also earned lower wages and didn't have access to the same benefits, like schools and healthcare, that the American workers did. This created a divide between the two groups, and while they worked together on the canal, their daily lives were quite separate.

Despite the challenges, many of the local workers were proud of the role they played in building and maintaining the canal. They knew they were part of something big, something that was changing the world.

The canal was a massive project, and it needed thousands of workers to dig, build, and operate it. The people who worked there were part of a global effort, and they knew that their work would be remembered for generations.

The Panama Canal Zone was also a place where cultures mixed. Workers from different countries brought their own traditions, languages, and foods, and this created a unique cultural environment. In the local markets, you could find foods from the Caribbean, Central America, and the United States. There were festivals and celebrations from different cultures, and people often shared their traditions with one another. While there were clear divisions between the different groups, the Panama Canal Zone was also a place where cultures came together in ways that you didn't see in many other places.

One of the most interesting things about life in the Panama Canal Zone was the connection to the canal itself. Almost everyone in the zone had some connection to the canal, whether they were working directly on it or supporting the people who did. The canal was the reason the zone existed, and it was a constant presence in people's lives. The giant ships passing through the locks, the sound of machinery, and the sight of the water rising and falling were part of daily life. Even kids growing up in the zone understood how important the canal was. They learned about it in school, they saw it every day, and some of them even dreamed of working on it when they grew up.

The Panama Canal also brought a sense of purpose and pride to the people who lived in the zone. They knew that the canal was one of the most important engineering feats in history and that it was changing the way the world worked. Ships from all over the globe passed through the canal, carrying goods and people between the Atlantic and Pacific Oceans. The workers in the zone played a key role in keeping the canal running smoothly, and they took pride in the fact that they were part of something so significant.

But life in the Panama Canal Zone wasn't always easy. The climate was tough, with hot temperatures, heavy rains, and thick humidity. There were also dangers, especially for the workers who had to clear the land, dig through mountains, and build the locks. Disease was a constant threat, with mosquitoes carrying deadly illnesses like malaria and yellow fever. While public health campaigns had reduced the spread of these diseases, they hadn't been completely eliminated, and workers still had to be careful.

Despite these challenges, many people who lived and worked in the Panama Canal Zone felt like they were part of something special. They were living in a place that was at the center of global trade and world history. The canal zone was not just a job site; it was a community, a place where people raised their families, made friends, and built their lives. It was a place where cultures came together, where people from different backgrounds worked side by side on one of the greatest engineering projects of all time.

Even after the canal was completed in 1914, life in the Panama Canal Zone continued to revolve around the canal. The workers who operated the locks, maintained the machinery, and ensured that ships could pass through safely were just as important as the workers who had built the canal. The canal zone remained under U.S. control until 1979, and during that time, it continued to function like a little piece of America in the middle of Panama. For many people who lived there, the canal zone was more than just a place to work—it was home.

In the end, life in the Panama Canal Zone was about much more than just building and operating the canal. It was about community, culture, and the connections between people. It was a place where people from different parts of the world came together to work on a project that would change the course of history. And for the people who lived there, the Panama Canal Zone was a place where they could be part of something bigger than themselves, something that would be remembered for generations to come.

Chapter 10: The French Effort to Build the Canal

Before the Panama Canal became one of the greatest engineering achievements of the 20th century, there was another attempt to build it by the French in the late 1800s. The French effort to build the canal is a fascinating and dramatic chapter in history. It was filled with ambition, hope, and ultimately, failure. But this failure wasn't because the French lacked skill or vision. Instead, it was the result of many unexpected and overwhelming challenges that no one could have anticipated. The story of the French attempt to build the Panama Canal is a tale of great ambition, incredible hardship, and lessons that paved the way for the eventual success of the project.

The French effort to build the Panama Canal began in the 1880s, and at the time, the world was still amazed by the Suez Canal, which had been completed in 1869. The Suez Canal was a massive success, connecting the Mediterranean Sea to the Red Sea and dramatically shortening the sea route between Europe and Asia. It had been built under the leadership of Ferdinand de Lesseps, a French diplomat and engineer who was hailed as a hero for his achievement. After the success of the Suez Canal, de Lesseps was determined to build another canal, this time connecting the Atlantic and Pacific Oceans through Central America. He believed that this canal, like the Suez Canal, would revolutionize global trade and solidify France's position as a world leader in engineering.

De Lesseps was confident that if he could build the Suez Canal, he could build a canal in Panama. However, the two canals were very different projects. The Suez Canal was built through flat desert terrain, and it was a sea-level canal, meaning that ships could sail straight through without needing to be lifted or lowered. The Panama Canal, on the other hand, would need to be built through dense jungle and mountainous terrain. It also required a different type of engineering solution, as the elevation of the land in Panama made a sea-level canal extremely difficult. But de Lesseps believed that the same principles that had worked in Suez would work in Panama, so he moved forward with his plan.

In 1879, de Lesseps organized an international conference to gather support for the Panama Canal project. He convinced investors and the French government to back the project, raising millions of dollars to fund the construction. He also formed the Compagnie Universelle du Canal Interocéanique de Panama (Universal Company of the Interoceanic Canal of Panama) to oversee the work. With financial backing and an experienced team of engineers, de Lesseps was ready to begin what he thought would be another triumph of French engineering.

But almost from the beginning, the French effort to build the Panama Canal ran into serious problems. The first challenge was the geography of Panama itself. The terrain was much more difficult than anyone had anticipated. The canal would have to cut through the dense jungle, which was full of thick vegetation, dangerous wildlife, and steep mountains. The most formidable obstacle was the Culebra Cut, a massive section of the Panamanian mountains that would need to be dug through to create a path for the canal. This was a huge challenge for the engineers, as they had never dealt with anything on this scale before.

On top of the difficult terrain, the weather in Panama was brutal. The region experienced heavy rainfall for much of the year, which caused landslides and flooding, making it nearly impossible for the workers to make steady progress. The heat and humidity were oppressive, and many workers struggled to adapt to the harsh conditions. Unlike in the Suez Canal project, where the desert was dry and stable, the rain-soaked jungle of Panama constantly shifted, creating dangerous working conditions.

But perhaps the biggest challenge faced by the French was disease. Panama was home to swarms of mosquitoes that carried deadly diseases like malaria and yellow fever. These diseases spread quickly among the workers, killing thousands. At the time, people didn't understand how these diseases were transmitted, so there was no way to protect the workers from getting sick. The French workers had come to Panama full of optimism, but soon the construction sites turned into makeshift hospitals, with sick workers lying in hammocks, too weak to continue working. The death toll was staggering—an estimated 22,000 workers died during the French attempt to build the canal. This was not only a human tragedy, but it also severely slowed down the progress of the construction.

In addition to the disease and difficult working conditions, the French project also suffered from poor planning and management. De Lesseps was not an engineer by training; he was a diplomat and a visionary. He had successfully overseen the construction of the Suez Canal, but the conditions in Panama were entirely different, and his lack of engineering expertise became a problem. He insisted on building a sea-level canal, just like in Suez, even though his engineers warned him that this would be nearly impossible in Panama due to the mountains. Building a sea-level canal would require an enormous amount of digging, far more than had been needed in Suez, and the constant landslides made this task even more daunting.

Despite the mounting problems, de Lesseps remained optimistic and pushed forward. He believed that with enough money and manpower, the canal could still be completed. But as the years went on and the project continued to face setbacks, the costs began to spiral out of control. Investors who had initially been excited about the project began to lose confidence, and the French company started running out of money. The financial strain, combined with the high death toll and slow progress, eventually led to the collapse of the project.

In 1889, after nearly a decade of struggling to build the canal, the French company went bankrupt. The dream of a French-built canal through Panama was over. The failure was a huge embarrassment for France, and it became one of the biggest financial scandals of the time. Thousands of people had invested their savings in the canal project, and when it failed, many of them lost everything. De Lesseps himself, once a national hero, was disgraced. He was put on trial for fraud, along with several other key figures in the project, and although he was convicted, he never went to prison due to his advanced age.

The failure of the French effort to build the Panama Canal left a massive unfinished project in the jungle. Equipment, buildings, and partially dug sections of the canal were abandoned, and for years, the site remained a sad reminder of what could have been. But while the French effort had ended in failure, it was not entirely in vain. The French had done important work in surveying the land, mapping out a possible route for the canal, and beginning the excavation. They had also learned valuable lessons about the challenges of building a canal in Panama, lessons that would later be crucial when the Americans took over the project.

One of the most important contributions of the French effort was the realization that a sea-level canal was not practical in Panama. This paved the way for the eventual decision to build a canal with locks, which allowed ships to be raised and lowered as they passed through the canal. This was a much more feasible solution given the terrain, and it became the key to the successful completion of the canal.

The French also brought attention to the issue of disease in Panama. While they were unable to solve the problem, their experience showed just how deadly yellow fever and malaria could be. When the Americans took over the project years later, they made it a priority to tackle the issue of disease, and their success in controlling yellow fever and malaria was one of the key reasons the canal was eventually completed.

In many ways, the French effort to build the Panama Canal was a story of great ambition that was undone by forces beyond anyone's control. The terrain, the climate, and the disease were all far more difficult to overcome than anyone had imagined. But even though the French failed to complete the canal, their work laid the foundation for the American effort that would come later. The dream of connecting the Atlantic and Pacific Oceans didn't die with the French failure—it simply passed on to the next generation of engineers and workers.

Ferdinand de Lesseps, despite the failure in Panama, is still remembered as a visionary. His success with the Suez Canal had shown the world what was possible, and even though his attempt to build the Panama Canal didn't succeed, it inspired others to continue the effort. The French effort may have ended in defeat, but it played a crucial role in the eventual triumph of the Panama Canal, one of the greatest engineering feats in history.

Today, when ships pass through the Panama Canal, they follow a route that was first surveyed by the French engineers. The canal that the French dreamed of was finally built, not by them, but with the help of the lessons they had learned. The French effort to build the canal was a stepping stone to its ultimate success, showing that even failure can lead to great achievements in the future.

Chapter 11: The Importance of the Panama Canal Today

The Panama Canal is one of the most important waterways in the world today, even though it was built more than a century ago. Its importance has only grown over time, as the canal plays a crucial role in global trade, connecting the Atlantic and Pacific Oceans. This shortcut across Central America allows ships to avoid the long and dangerous journey around the southern tip of South America, at Cape Horn, which is one of the most treacherous routes in the world. By saving time and distance, the Panama Canal has helped to make global shipping faster, more efficient, and more affordable. But the importance of the Panama Canal goes beyond just trade—it affects economies, politics, and even the environment in ways that many people may not realize.

First, the Panama Canal is incredibly important for international trade. Every day, huge cargo ships pass through the canal, carrying goods from one side of the world to the other. These ships transport all kinds of products, from cars and electronics to food and clothing. The canal allows these goods to move more quickly between markets, which means that businesses can operate more efficiently, and consumers can get products faster and at lower costs. Without the Panama Canal, many of the goods that people use every day would take much longer to arrive, and they would likely be more expensive because of the increased shipping costs. In this way, the canal helps to keep the global economy moving smoothly.

The canal also plays a huge role in the economies of many countries. For Panama, the canal is one of the country's most valuable assets. Since Panama regained control of the canal from the United States in 1999, it has become a major source of income for the country. The fees that ships pay to pass through the canal bring in billions of dollars every year, which helps fund infrastructure, education, and healthcare in Panama. In fact, the canal is such a vital part of Panama's economy that it's often seen as a symbol of the country's independence and success. Beyond Panama, many other countries also benefit from the canal because it allows their exports and imports to move more efficiently. For example, countries that rely on trade, such as the United States, China, and countries in Europe, all depend on the Panama Canal to keep their goods flowing smoothly.

The Panama Canal also plays an important role in international relations and politics. Because the canal is such a key part of global trade, it has often been at the center of international negotiations and agreements. When the canal was controlled by the United States, it was a source of tension between the U.S. and Panama, as many Panamanians felt that the canal should belong to them. This led to years of negotiations, which eventually resulted in the U.S. agreeing to hand over control of the canal to Panama in 1999. Since then, Panama has successfully managed the canal, and its operation has remained peaceful and stable, which is crucial for the countries that rely on it. Today, the Panama Canal is seen as an example of how countries can cooperate to manage important global resources.

The Panama Canal is also vital to the global shipping industry. Ships are designed with the canal in mind, and many are built to fit the exact dimensions of the canal's locks. These ships are called "Panamax" ships, and they are the largest size that can fit through the original locks of the canal. In recent years, however, the global shipping industry has changed. Ships have become larger, and the demand for transporting goods has increased. To keep up with this demand, the Panama Canal underwent a major expansion, which was completed in 2016. This expansion added a new set of larger locks, called the "Neo-Panamax" locks, which allow much bigger ships to pass through the canal. These larger ships can carry more cargo, which makes shipping even more efficient and helps reduce costs for businesses and consumers around the world.

The expansion of the Panama Canal has had a huge impact on global trade. Before the expansion, many of the largest ships in the world couldn't fit through the canal and had to take longer routes, such as around the southern tip of South America or through the Suez Canal in Egypt. But now, with the new locks, these larger ships can pass through Panama, saving time and fuel. This has made the canal even more important for international shipping, and it has increased the number of ships that use the canal every year.

Another reason the Panama Canal is so important today is because it helps reduce the environmental impact of global shipping. When ships take shorter routes, like through the canal, they burn less fuel, which means they produce fewer emissions. This is important because the shipping industry is one of the largest contributors to global greenhouse gas emissions. By providing a more direct route between the Atlantic and Pacific Oceans, the Panama Canal helps to reduce the amount of pollution that ships produce. In this way, the canal plays a small but important role in helping to protect the environment.

The Panama Canal is also important for national security, especially for countries like the United States. Because the canal connects two major oceans, it allows military ships to move more quickly between the Atlantic and Pacific. This is especially important during times of conflict or crisis, when military forces need to be able to respond quickly to threats. The ability to move ships and equipment through the canal can give countries a strategic advantage, which is why the canal has always been viewed as a key military asset.

In addition to its economic, political, and environmental importance, the Panama Canal is also an incredible engineering marvel. It represents one of the greatest feats of human ingenuity and determination. The canal took over 10 years to build and required the efforts of tens of thousands of workers from all over the world. The challenges they faced—including digging through mountains, dealing with deadly diseases, and managing the difficult terrain—were enormous, yet they persevered. The result is a waterway that continues to serve as a vital link in the global transportation network. Today, engineers and tourists alike marvel at the Panama Canal's system of locks, which raise and lower ships over the 85-foot difference between the Atlantic and Pacific Oceans. The canal's innovative design and engineering are still admired today as one of the most remarkable accomplishments in history.

In recent years, the importance of the Panama Canal has continued to grow as global trade increases. More goods are being shipped across the world than ever before, and the Panama Canal remains a key route for much of that trade. As more countries participate in global commerce, the demand for efficient shipping routes like the Panama Canal will only increase. The canal is expected to play an even bigger role in the future as trade between Asia and the Americas continues to grow.

But with this growing importance comes new challenges. The Panama Canal faces the threat of climate change, which could have a major impact on its operations. Rising sea levels, changes in rainfall patterns, and other environmental changes could affect the canal's ability to function. For example, the canal relies on fresh water from nearby lakes to operate its locks, and if rainfall decreases, it could create a shortage of water, making it difficult to raise and lower ships. Panama is already working on solutions to these problems, such as finding ways to conserve water and improve the canal's efficiency. But as the climate continues to change, it will be important for Panama and the global community to work together to ensure that the canal remains a reliable and efficient part of the world's shipping system.

In conclusion, the Panama Canal is more than just a shortcut between two oceans. It is a vital part of the global economy, a key element of international trade, and an engineering marvel that continues to inspire people around the world. Its ability to save time, reduce costs, and connect different parts of the world has made it one of the most important waterways in history. As global trade continues to expand, and as the world faces new challenges, the Panama Canal's role will remain crucial. Its importance today, more than 100 years after it was built, is a testament to the vision and determination of the people who created it and to the ongoing efforts to keep it running smoothly in the modern world.

Chapter 12: How the Panama Canal Changed Global Trade

The Panama Canal revolutionized global trade in ways that are still being felt today, more than 100 years after it was first built. Before the canal was completed, moving goods between the Atlantic and Pacific Oceans was a difficult, time-consuming, and expensive task. Ships had to sail all the way around the southern tip of South America, through the treacherous waters of Cape Horn, which added thousands of miles to their journey. This long and dangerous route made global trade slower and less efficient, which in turn affected the prices of goods and how quickly they could reach their destinations. The opening of the Panama Canal in 1914 changed all of that. It created a shortcut between the two oceans, dramatically reducing travel time, fuel costs, and making global trade faster, cheaper, and more accessible to countries all over the world.

One of the most significant ways that the Panama Canal changed global trade was by cutting down the distance that ships had to travel. Before the canal, ships sailing from New York to San Francisco, for example, had to take a route that was over 13,000 miles long. They had to go all the way down the eastern coast of the Americas, around the tip of South America, and then back up the western coast. This journey took weeks or even months, depending on weather conditions. But with the Panama Canal, ships could pass straight through Central America, reducing the distance to just 5,200 miles. This shorter route saved time, fuel, and money, which allowed businesses to move goods more quickly and efficiently. For many companies, the savings from using the Panama Canal meant they could lower their costs and offer more competitive prices, making their products more attractive to buyers around the world.

The canal's impact wasn't just about saving time and money—it also opened up new opportunities for trade. By providing a direct route between the Atlantic and Pacific Oceans, the canal made it easier for countries on opposite sides of the world to do business with each other. For example, it allowed goods from the east coast of the United States to be shipped more easily to markets in Asia and vice versa. This expanded trade networks and helped to create a truly global marketplace, where goods could flow more freely between continents. In this way, the Panama Canal played a key role in the development of the global economy, helping to bring the world closer together through trade.

Another major impact of the Panama Canal was the way it affected the shipping industry. Before the canal, many companies had to make difficult decisions about how to transport their goods. For example, some companies chose to ship their products across land, using trains to carry goods between the east and west coasts of the United States. This was faster than sailing around South America, but it was also expensive and limited the amount of goods that could be transported. The Panama Canal changed this by making sea travel more efficient and affordable. Ships could now carry much larger quantities of goods directly between oceans, bypassing the need for overland transportation. This made shipping by sea the preferred method of transporting goods, which had a huge impact on the global economy.

The canal also had a transformative effect on the kinds of ships that were built. With the opening of the canal, shipbuilders started designing vessels specifically to fit through its locks. These ships, known as "Panamax" ships, were built to the maximum size that could pass through the canal's original locks, which were 110 feet wide, 1,000 feet long, and 41 feet deep. This led to the creation of a new standard in ship design, with Panamax ships becoming the workhorses of global trade. These ships could carry more cargo than smaller vessels, which made them more efficient and cost-effective for transporting goods.

As global trade grew, the demand for larger ships increased, and the Panama Canal helped shape the future of the shipping industry by setting the standard for ship sizes.

Over time, as global trade continued to expand, the limitations of the original Panama Canal became apparent. Larger ships were being built, and many of them could not fit through the canal's locks. This led to the development of even bigger ships, known as "post-Panamax" or "Neo-Panamax" ships, which could carry even more cargo. However, these ships had to take alternate routes because they were too big for the Panama Canal. This created a demand for a new solution, and in 2016, the Panama Canal underwent a massive expansion. The expansion added a new set of locks, called the Neo-Panamax locks, which were wider, longer, and deeper than the original ones. This allowed much larger ships to pass through the canal, further increasing its importance for global trade.

The expansion of the Panama Canal had a huge impact on global shipping. Larger ships could now carry more goods in a single trip, which reduced costs for shipping companies and made trade even more efficient. This also allowed for the transportation of more diverse types of cargo, such as liquefied natural gas (LNG), which had previously been difficult to transport through the canal. The expansion also opened up new markets and trade routes, particularly for countries in Asia and the Americas. For example, ships carrying goods from China to the east coast of the United States could now pass through the canal, rather than taking the longer route around South America or through the Suez Canal. This made trade between Asia and the Americas faster and more affordable, benefiting businesses and consumers in both regions.

In addition to making shipping more efficient, the Panama Canal has also played a critical role in shaping the economies of many countries. For Panama itself, the canal is a major source of revenue. The fees that ships pay to use the canal are a significant part of the country's economy, and the canal's success has helped to improve infrastructure, healthcare, and education in Panama. The canal has also created jobs for thousands of Panamanians, both directly through its operation and indirectly through the businesses that support it. For countries that rely heavily on exports, such as the United States, China, and many countries in Latin America, the Panama Canal has been crucial in helping them reach global markets more easily and efficiently.

Another important way the Panama Canal has changed global trade is by promoting greater economic cooperation between countries. Because the canal is such a vital part of international shipping, many countries have a vested interest in ensuring that it operates smoothly and efficiently. This has led to greater cooperation between countries that use the canal and Panama, as they work together to keep the canal running safely and efficiently. In some cases, the canal has even helped to ease tensions between countries by providing a neutral ground where they can work together to achieve common goals. For example, the canal has been used as a strategic route for military vessels during times of conflict, helping to promote peace and security in the region.

The Panama Canal has also had a significant impact on the environment. By providing a shorter route for ships, the canal helps to reduce the amount of fuel that ships burn, which in turn reduces greenhouse gas emissions. This is important because the shipping industry is one of the largest contributors to global carbon emissions. By allowing ships to take a more direct route, the Panama Canal helps to reduce the environmental impact of global trade. However, the canal also faces challenges related to the environment. Climate change poses a threat to the canal's operation, as rising sea levels, changes in rainfall patterns, and other environmental factors could affect its ability to function. For example, the canal relies on fresh water from nearby lakes to operate its locks, and if there is less rainfall, it could create a shortage of water, making it difficult to raise and lower ships. Panama is already working on solutions to these problems, such as finding ways to conserve water and improve the canal's efficiency.

One of the long-term effects of the Panama Canal on global trade has been the way it has shaped the flow of goods around the world. Before the canal, certain trade routes were more dominant, such as those that went through Europe or around the southern tip of Africa. But with the opening of the Panama Canal, new trade routes emerged, particularly between the Americas and Asia. This has helped to shift the balance of global trade, making countries in the Western Hemisphere more important players in the global economy. The canal has also helped to reduce the dominance of European trade routes, as goods can now be shipped more easily between other parts of the world.

In conclusion, the Panama Canal has had an enormous impact on global trade. By providing a shorter, more efficient route between the Atlantic and Pacific Oceans, the canal has helped to reduce shipping costs, open up new trade opportunities, and shape the future of the global shipping industry. The expansion of the canal has further increased its importance, allowing larger ships to pass through and making trade even more efficient. The canal has also played a key role in shaping the economies of many countries, promoting economic cooperation, and reducing the environmental impact of global trade. Today, the Panama Canal remains one of the most important waterways in the world, and its influence on global trade is likely to continue for many years to come.

Chapter 13: Animals and Nature Around the Canal

The Panama Canal is not just an engineering marvel—it's also surrounded by one of the most incredible natural environments on Earth. The region around the canal is home to a wide variety of animals, plants, and ecosystems that make it one of the most biodiverse areas in the world. Because the canal cuts through the narrowest part of Central America, it serves as a natural corridor, linking the Atlantic and Pacific Oceans. This unique geographic location allows different species to travel and thrive, creating a diverse landscape of jungles, rainforests, rivers, and wetlands. The construction of the canal had a significant impact on the environment, but despite this, the area remains rich in wildlife and natural beauty. Today, the region around the canal is not only vital for global shipping but also for the preservation of many endangered species and unique ecosystems.

The tropical rainforest surrounding the Panama Canal is home to an amazing variety of animals. One of the most iconic creatures found in this region is the jaguar. Jaguars are the largest cats in the Americas and are known for their beautiful spotted coats. These powerful predators roam the dense forests, hunting animals like deer, peccaries (wild pigs), and smaller mammals. Jaguars are extremely elusive and rarely seen by people, but their presence is a sign of a healthy ecosystem. The area around the canal provides an important habitat for these big cats, as well as for other large predators like pumas and ocelots. These wild cats are part of a delicate balance in the food chain, helping to control populations of smaller animals and keeping the ecosystem in check.

The forests around the Panama Canal are also teeming with monkeys. Several species of monkeys live in the treetops, including howler monkeys, capuchins, and spider monkeys. Howler monkeys are known for their incredibly loud calls, which can be heard for miles through the jungle. These calls help them communicate with other members of their group and establish their territory. Capuchin monkeys are smaller and highly intelligent; they are often seen using tools like sticks and rocks to find food. Spider monkeys, with their long, gangly limbs, swing gracefully through the trees in search of fruit. These monkeys play an important role in the ecosystem by spreading seeds through the forest, which helps trees and plants grow.

One of the most fascinating animals found near the canal is the sloth. Sloths are famous for their slow, deliberate movements and for spending most of their time hanging upside down in trees. They move so slowly that algae often grow on their fur, giving them a greenish tint that helps them blend in with the leaves. There are two types of sloths in the region: the two-toed sloth and the three-toed sloth. Sloths are perfectly adapted to life in the treetops, where they eat leaves and occasionally venture down to the ground to find water or a new tree to live in. These gentle creatures are a favorite of visitors to the area, and spotting a sloth in the wild is always a special treat.

The Panama Canal area is also a paradise for birdwatchers. Over 900 species of birds have been recorded in the region, making it one of the most diverse bird habitats in the world. Brightly colored toucans, with their enormous beaks, are a common sight in the treetops. These birds eat fruit and are known for their playful, social behavior. Parrots and macaws, with their vivid feathers, can often be seen flying in flocks, filling the sky with bursts of color. Many species of hummingbirds also live in the area, flitting from flower to flower in search of nectar. The forests around the canal are a crucial habitat for these birds, many of which are migratory and depend on the area for food and shelter during their long journeys between North and South America.

The waters around the Panama Canal are just as rich in life as the forests. The canal itself is connected to the Chagres River, one of the most important rivers in Panama, which flows into Gatun Lake, a large man-made lake that was created during the construction of the canal. Gatun Lake is now a vital part of the canal system, but it is also home to an abundance of aquatic life. Fish like the tarpon, snook, and peacock bass thrive in these waters, attracting both local fishermen and visitors. The lake is also a habitat for crocodiles, which can often be seen basking on the banks or swimming just beneath the surface. These reptiles are top predators in the water and help maintain the balance of the aquatic ecosystem.

In addition to crocodiles, another fascinating reptile found in the region is the green iguana. These large, tree-dwelling lizards can often be seen sunning themselves on branches or rocks near the water. Green iguanas are herbivores, meaning they eat plants, and they play a role in controlling vegetation in the area. They are excellent climbers and swimmers, and their bright green coloration helps them blend in with the jungle foliage. The canal zone is also home to several species of turtles, both aquatic and land-based. These turtles lay their eggs on the banks of rivers and lakes, and their presence is a sign of a healthy aquatic environment.

Insects are another important part of the natural world around the Panama Canal. The warm, humid climate provides the perfect environment for a wide variety of insects, including butterflies, beetles, ants, and mosquitoes. One of the most famous insects found in this region is the blue morpho butterfly. With its large, iridescent blue wings, the blue morpho is one of the most striking butterflies in the world. It can often be seen fluttering through the forest, where it feeds on the juices of rotting fruit. Other insects, like leafcutter ants, are vital to the ecosystem. Leafcutter ants carry pieces of leaves back to their underground nests, where they use the leaves to cultivate fungus, which they eat. These ants are incredible workers and can carry pieces of leaves that are much larger than their own bodies.

One of the greatest challenges facing the animals and nature around the Panama Canal is habitat loss. The construction of the canal and the development of surrounding areas have led to the destruction of large portions of the rainforest. This has reduced the amount of habitat available for many species, making it harder for them to find food and shelter. Deforestation and development also disrupt the delicate balance of the ecosystem, putting pressure on both plants and animals. In response to these challenges, conservation efforts have been put in place to protect the natural environment around the canal. Several national parks and reserves have been established to preserve the rainforest and provide a safe haven for wildlife. These protected areas are vital for the survival of many species and help to ensure that the region's incredible biodiversity is not lost.

Another environmental challenge related to the Panama Canal is water management. The canal relies on large amounts of fresh water from nearby lakes and rivers to operate its locks, which raise and lower ships as they pass through. However, the demand for water is increasing, both for the canal and for the growing population of Panama. This has led to concerns about water shortages, especially during dry seasons. If there is not enough water, it could affect both the operation of the canal and the health of the surrounding ecosystems. To address this issue, efforts are being made to manage water resources more efficiently and to find ways to reduce the canal's water usage without harming the environment.

Despite the challenges, the area around the Panama Canal remains a treasure trove of natural wonders. The combination of tropical rainforests, rivers, and lakes creates a diverse ecosystem that supports a wide variety of life, from the smallest insects to the largest predators. This biodiversity makes the canal zone one of the most important natural regions in the world, not just for the animals that live there, but also for scientists and researchers who study the region's unique ecosystems. The canal area is a living laboratory, where researchers can observe how animals and plants interact with each other and how they adapt to changes in their environment.

For visitors, the Panama Canal region offers an incredible opportunity to experience nature up close. Many guided tours and nature walks are available, allowing people to explore the rainforests, see the animals in their natural habitats, and learn about the efforts being made to protect the environment. Gatun Lake is a popular spot for eco-tours, where visitors can take boat rides to see wildlife such as monkeys, sloths, and exotic birds. The canal itself is also a draw for tourists, who can watch as massive ships are raised and lowered in the locks while surrounded by the lush greenery of the rainforest.

In conclusion, the Panama Canal is much more than just a passage for ships—it's a gateway to one of the most diverse and vibrant natural environments in the world. The animals and nature around the canal are a testament to the incredible biodiversity of the region, and they play a vital role in maintaining the health of the ecosystem. From jaguars and monkeys to birds, reptiles, and insects, the wildlife of the canal zone is as rich and varied as the canal itself is important for global trade. Despite the challenges of habitat loss and environmental pressures, conservation efforts are helping to preserve this unique region for future generations. The Panama Canal and its surrounding wilderness are not only a triumph of human engineering but also a reminder of the beauty and importance of the natural world.

Chapter 14: The Technology Behind the Canal's Locks

The technology behind the Panama Canal's locks is one of the most fascinating parts of this engineering marvel. The locks are what make the canal work. Without them, ships would not be able to cross from one ocean to the other. They allow ships to be lifted up and down over the rugged terrain and through the changing elevations of Panama. The canal spans more than 50 miles (80 kilometers) from the Atlantic to the Pacific Ocean, and the land it crosses isn't flat. In fact, at its highest point, the canal rises about 85 feet (26 meters) above sea level. To make this passage possible, engineers came up with an ingenious system of locks—massive chambers filled with water that raise and lower ships like giant elevators.

Let's start with what a lock is. A lock is essentially a watertight chamber that ships enter, and by controlling the flow of water in and out of the chamber, ships can be raised or lowered. The Panama Canal originally had three sets of locks: one on the Atlantic side at Gatun, one on the Pacific side at Miraflores, and another set at Pedro Miguel. Each lock chamber is 110 feet (33.5 meters) wide, 1,000 feet (305 meters) long, and 41 feet (12.5 meters) deep. These chambers are big enough to hold huge ships, which are known as Panamax vessels—named because they are the maximum size that can fit through the original locks.

The way the locks work is based on gravity, which means no pumps are needed to move water in and out of the chambers. Instead, water flows naturally from nearby lakes and reservoirs into the locks through a series of large culverts (tunnels). The water in the locks comes from Gatun Lake, which was created by damming the Chagres River. This man-made lake is essential to the canal's operation, as it provides the water needed to fill the locks and move ships up and down. Here's how it works: when a ship enters the lock, the gates are closed behind it, creating a watertight seal. Then, water is either added or drained from the chamber to raise or lower the ship to the next level.

The process of raising a ship in a lock works like this: first, the lock is filled with water until it reaches the same level as the next lock chamber, which is higher up. Water flows into the lock from the lake through large openings, filling the chamber and lifting the ship. As the water level rises, so does the ship, until it's at the same height as the next chamber. When the water level is equal, the gates open, and the ship moves forward to the next chamber. This process is repeated until the ship reaches the top level of the canal.

Once the ship has passed through the highest point of the canal, the process is reversed to lower it back down to sea level. In this case, instead of adding water to the lock, the water is drained out. Gravity pulls the water down into the lower chambers or back into the lake, and as the water level drops, so does the ship. When the water level is the same as the lower chamber, the gates open, and the ship moves forward. The process continues until the ship is lowered all the way back down to sea level on the other side of the canal. It takes about 8 to 10 hours for a ship to travel through the entire canal, but going through just one lock takes only about 30 minutes.

The gates of the locks are one of the most impressive parts of the system. Each gate is made of steel and weighs hundreds of tons, yet they are so well-balanced that they can be opened and closed with surprisingly little effort. The original gates were designed to last for a long time, and some of them have been in operation since the canal opened in 1914. The gates are hollow, which makes them strong yet light enough to be moved by electric motors. These motors control the movement of the gates and are operated from a control house, where operators carefully monitor the position of the ship and the water levels. It's crucial that the gates are operated with precision, as even a small mistake could lead to damage to the ship or the lock.

Another key part of the lock system is the mules, which are not actual animals but rather electric locomotives that help guide the ships through the locks. These mules run on tracks along the side of the locks and are attached to the ships by strong cables. Their job is to keep the ship steady and in the center of the lock chamber as it moves through. Ships are massive and can be difficult to maneuver, especially in the narrow space of the lock chamber, so the mules play a critical role in preventing collisions with the sides of the locks. Each ship is typically guided by multiple mules—two at the front and two at the back. The mules don't pull the ships through the locks; the ships move under their own power. The mules simply help to keep them straight and prevent them from hitting the walls.

In 2016, the Panama Canal underwent a major expansion, known as the Panama Canal Expansion or the Third Set of Locks project. This expansion was necessary because ships were getting bigger, and many modern vessels, known as post-Panamax ships, were too large to fit through the original locks. The new set of locks is called the Neo-Panamax locks, and they are much larger than the original ones. The new locks are 180 feet (55 meters) wide, 1,400 feet (427 meters) long, and 60 feet (18.3 meters) deep. These dimensions allow the canal to accommodate much larger ships, which can carry up to three times more cargo than the original Panamax vessels.

The technology behind the Neo-Panamax locks is even more advanced than the original locks. One of the most significant improvements is the use of water-saving basins. Unlike the original locks, where water flows directly from Gatun Lake into the locks, the new locks have special basins that capture and reuse water. This is important because operating the locks requires a huge amount of fresh water, and Panama experiences both wet and dry seasons. By recycling up to 60% of the water used in each lockage (the process of moving a ship through the locks), the new system conserves water and helps ensure that there is enough to keep the canal running year-round.

The gates of the Neo-Panamax locks are also different from the original gates. Instead of swinging open like a door, the new gates are rolling gates, which means they slide horizontally into the sides of the lock chamber. This design takes up less space and makes it easier to maintain the gates. The new gates are also much taller and heavier than the original ones, but they are designed to withstand the enormous pressure of the water and the weight of the larger ships that pass through. Like the original gates, the new gates are controlled by electric motors and are operated with great precision.

Another technological advancement in the new locks is the use of tugboats instead of mules to guide the ships. The larger post-Panamax ships are so big that the traditional mules would not be able to handle them. Instead, powerful tugboats are used to help guide the ships through the locks. These tugboats are positioned at the front and back of the ship and help to push and pull the vessel through the chamber, ensuring that it stays centered and doesn't hit the walls. The use of tugboats allows for greater flexibility and control, especially with the larger ships.

One of the most impressive aspects of the locks is how efficiently they operate. The entire process is carefully timed and coordinated to ensure that ships can move through the canal as quickly as possible. From the moment a ship approaches the locks, a team of operators takes over, guiding the vessel through each step of the process. The ship's speed, position, and water levels are all monitored in real time from control towers, and adjustments are made as needed to ensure a smooth passage. Even though the system is over 100 years old, it remains remarkably efficient and reliable.

In addition to the mechanical and electrical systems that control the locks, modern technology plays a role in monitoring and maintaining the canal. Sensors and cameras are used to keep track of the condition of the locks, the gates, and the surrounding infrastructure. This allows engineers to identify any potential issues before they become serious problems. Regular maintenance is essential to keep the locks in working order, and the canal has a dedicated team of workers who perform routine inspections, repairs, and upgrades. This ongoing maintenance is one of the reasons the canal has been able to operate continuously for more than a century.

The locks of the Panama Canal are not only an engineering triumph but also a testament to human ingenuity. The technology behind them, from the clever use of gravity to the precision machinery that operates the gates, has stood the test of time. Even as the world has changed and ships have grown larger, the basic principles behind the locks remain the same. The expansion of the canal and the addition of the Neo-Panamax locks show that this technology can evolve to meet new challenges while continuing to play a vital role in global trade. Today, the Panama Canal is one of the most important waterways in the world, and its locks are the heart of its success.

Chapter 15: The Workers Who Built the Panama Canal

The story of the workers who built the Panama Canal is one of incredible determination, hard work, and sacrifice. Thousands of men and women from all over the world came to Panama to help construct what would become one of the greatest engineering achievements in history. Building the canal was a massive and dangerous undertaking, and the workers faced countless challenges along the way. They battled extreme heat, tropical diseases, and difficult working conditions, but their dedication and perseverance made the canal a reality. Without their hard work, the canal would never have been completed, and the world might have looked very different today.

The workers who built the Panama Canal came from many different countries and backgrounds. While some of the workers were from the United States, where the canal project was managed after the French effort failed, the majority of the labor force came from the Caribbean, especially from islands like Jamaica, Barbados, and Trinidad. These men were known as "West Indians," and they made up the largest group of workers on the canal. Other workers came from places like Europe, Asia, and even Africa. It was a truly international workforce, and people of many different nationalities worked side by side to dig the canal.

The canal workers faced incredibly harsh conditions, especially in the early years of construction. Panama's climate is tropical, meaning it's very hot and humid, and the region receives a lot of rain, especially during the wet season. The heat was unbearable for many workers, who had to spend long hours outside, digging, blasting through mountains, and moving dirt and rocks. Many workers suffered from heat exhaustion and dehydration, and it was common for people to collapse on the job. In addition to the heat, the work itself was physically demanding. The canal workers used shovels, pickaxes, and dynamite to dig through the rugged terrain. They worked long hours, often from sunrise to sunset, with very few breaks.

One of the biggest dangers the workers faced was disease. When the French first attempted to build the canal in the late 1800s, one of the reasons they failed was because so many workers died from diseases like malaria and yellow fever. These diseases were spread by mosquitoes, which were abundant in Panama's jungles and wetlands. The workers had very little protection against these illnesses, and many became sick and died. Malaria, which is spread by mosquitoes that carry the parasite in their bites, causes fever, chills, and severe fatigue. Yellow fever, another mosquito-borne illness, caused high fevers, vomiting, and, in severe cases, internal bleeding. Both diseases were deadly, and they took the lives of thousands of canal workers.

In the early 1900s, when the United States took over the canal project, one of the first things they did was address the problem of disease. Dr. William Gorgas, an American doctor, led a massive effort to control the spread of malaria and yellow fever by reducing the mosquito population. His team drained swamps, sprayed insecticides, and cleared brush where mosquitoes liked to breed. They also installed screens on windows and provided workers with better housing to protect them from mosquito bites. Thanks to these efforts, the number of workers who died from disease dropped dramatically, and the canal project was able to move forward.

Another major challenge the workers faced was the difficult terrain. The route of the canal passed through mountains, jungles, and swamps, which made the work incredibly difficult. One of the most daunting tasks was cutting through the Culebra Cut, a nine-mile stretch of mountainous terrain that had to be dug out to create the canal. Workers used dynamite to blast through the mountains, but this was extremely dangerous. Explosions were unpredictable, and workers had to be careful not to be caught in the blast. Despite the precautions, accidents happened, and many workers were killed or injured in explosions. In addition to the danger of dynamite, the area was prone to landslides. The loose soil and rocks often collapsed, burying workers and equipment under tons of debris.

The workers who built the Panama Canal also had to deal with long hours and harsh working conditions. Most of the manual laborers, particularly those from the Caribbean, were paid very little for their work. They earned just a few cents an hour and were often housed in overcrowded, unsanitary barracks. These workers were part of what was known as the "silver roll" system, which referred to the lower-wage workers, who were paid in silver. They were segregated from the higher-wage workers, who were mostly American and European, and were paid in gold, hence the name "gold roll." The gold roll workers had better living conditions, including access to nicer housing and better medical care. This system of segregation created tension between different groups of workers and highlighted the inequalities that existed on the canal project.

Despite these challenges, the workers persevered, and their efforts gradually began to pay off. By the time the canal was completed in 1914, more than 56,000 workers had been involved in the construction, and they had moved over 200 million cubic yards of earth and rock. This massive amount of material was dug out by hand, with the help of shovels, pickaxes, and dynamite, as well as by steam shovels and other machinery. The workers also built the canal's locks, which were made of massive concrete chambers designed to raise and lower ships. Constructing these locks was an enormous task that required a lot of skill and precision, and many workers spent years just on that part of the canal.

While the workers played a crucial role in the canal's construction, their contributions were not always properly recognized. Many of the Caribbean workers, who did some of the hardest and most dangerous labor, were not given the same credit as the American and European engineers who oversaw the project. In fact, after the canal was completed, many of these workers were forced to leave Panama, even though they had spent years helping to build the canal. They were seen as temporary laborers, and once their work was finished, they were no longer needed. This treatment caused a lot of resentment, especially among the West Indian workers, who felt they had been unfairly treated.

Life for the canal workers wasn't all about work, though. Despite the harsh conditions, many of the workers found ways to build a sense of community and enjoy life in Panama. The West Indian workers, for example, brought their own music, food, and culture with them to the canal zone. They would often gather in the evenings to play music, sing, and dance, creating a lively atmosphere despite the challenges they faced during the day. Their contributions to the culture of Panama can still be felt today, as many of their descendants continue to live in the country and have helped shape its cultural identity.

The role of women in the construction of the Panama Canal is also an important part of the story. While the majority of the workers were men, some women were involved in the project as well. Many women worked as cooks, laundresses, and nurses, helping to care for the male workers and providing essential support services. In particular, the nurses played a crucial role in caring for the sick and injured, especially those who contracted diseases like malaria and yellow fever. Without the work of these women, the canal workers would have had a much harder time surviving the harsh conditions.

By the time the Panama Canal was finished in 1914, it was clear that the workers had achieved something truly remarkable. They had overcome tremendous odds to build a waterway that would change the world forever. The canal allowed ships to travel between the Atlantic and Pacific Oceans without having to go around the southern tip of South America, saving both time and money. It also helped establish the United States as a major global power, as the U.S. controlled the canal for most of the 20th century. The workers who built the canal made all of this possible, and their legacy lives on today in the millions of ships that pass through the canal each year.

Even though the canal was completed more than a century ago, the workers' contributions are still remembered. Today, there are memorials and museums dedicated to the people who built the canal, and their stories are taught in schools and shared with visitors to Panama. Many of the descendants of the canal workers still live in Panama, especially in areas near the canal zone, and they are proud of the role their ancestors played in building this incredible structure. The Panama Canal stands as a testament to the hard work, ingenuity, and perseverance of the workers who made it possible.

In conclusion, the workers who built the Panama Canal were the backbone of the entire project. They came from different countries and backgrounds, but they all shared the common goal of completing one of the most ambitious engineering projects in history. They faced extreme heat, disease, difficult working conditions, and dangerous tasks, yet they persevered and succeeded in building a canal that would change the world. Their hard work and sacrifices made the Panama Canal a reality, and their legacy continues to be remembered and honored today.

Chapter 16: The Expansion of the Panama Canal

The expansion of the Panama Canal, known as the Panama Canal Expansion or the "Third Set of Locks" project, is one of the most significant engineering feats of modern times. This massive project, completed in 2016, transformed the Panama Canal, allowing it to accommodate much larger ships and ensuring that it could continue to meet the needs of global trade in the 21st century. The expansion was necessary because, since the canal first opened in 1914, ships had been getting bigger and bigger, and many of the largest vessels, known as "post-Panamax" ships, had outgrown the canal's original locks. These new, larger ships carried more cargo, but they couldn't fit through the narrow, 110-foot-wide (33.5 meters) locks of the original canal. The expansion changed all that, allowing the canal to handle much larger ships, which, in turn, has had a huge impact on global trade.

The expansion project was an enormous and complex undertaking. It involved building a new set of locks on both the Atlantic and Pacific sides of the canal that were much larger than the original ones. These new locks—referred to as the Neo-Panamax or post-Panamax locks—are 180 feet wide (55 meters), 1,400 feet long (427 meters), and 60 feet deep (18.3 meters). That's significantly bigger than the original locks, which are 110 feet wide, 1,000 feet long, and 41 feet deep. With these larger dimensions, the canal can now accommodate ships that are up to 1,200 feet long (366 meters) and 160 feet wide (49 meters)—ships that are more than twice the size of the largest vessels that could pass through the canal before the expansion. These new ships can carry up to 14,000 containers, compared to the 5,000 containers that fit on a Panamax ship, the maximum-sized vessel for the original locks.

The expansion project was first proposed in the late 20th century, as global shipping patterns began to change and larger ships became more common. The canal, which had been an essential shortcut for trade between the Atlantic and Pacific Oceans for most of the 20th century, was becoming less competitive because many of the largest ships had to take longer routes around the southern tip of South America, or through the Suez Canal, to get from one ocean to the other. Shipbuilders were designing larger vessels to transport more cargo in a single trip, which lowered shipping costs and made trade more efficient. But the Panama Canal's original locks were too small to handle these enormous ships. Recognizing that the canal was at risk of becoming outdated, the Panama Canal Authority (ACP) proposed a plan to expand the canal.

In 2006, the people of Panama voted in a national referendum to approve the expansion project, which was estimated to cost $5.25 billion. The expansion would involve several major components: building two new sets of locks—one on the Atlantic side at Agua Clara and one on the Pacific side at Cocolí; creating new access channels to connect the locks with the rest of the canal; widening and deepening existing navigation channels; and raising the level of Gatun Lake, the massive artificial lake that supplies water to the locks and forms part of the canal's route. These changes would not only allow larger ships to pass through the canal, but they would also improve the canal's overall efficiency and capacity.

Construction on the expansion began in 2007, and it took nearly a decade to complete. One of the most impressive parts of the project was the construction of the new locks. Each of the new locks consists of three chambers, just like the original locks, but these chambers are much larger. The new locks use a system of rolling gates, which slide horizontally into the lock walls, rather than the traditional swinging gates used in the original locks. These gates are massive, standing more than 90 feet tall (27 meters) and weighing over 3,000 tons each. The rolling design is not only more space-efficient, but it also allows for easier maintenance and operation.

Another key innovation in the new locks is the water-saving basins. One of the biggest challenges in operating the Panama Canal is managing the water supply. The locks require a huge amount of fresh water to lift and lower ships, and all of that water comes from Gatun Lake, which is fed by rainfall in Panama's tropical rainforest. During the dry season, water levels in the lake can drop, and there's always a concern that there might not be enough water to operate the locks. To address this issue, the new locks were designed with water-saving basins that allow 60% of the water used in each lockage to be recycled. These basins capture water that would otherwise be lost and pump it back into the lock system, reducing the overall water consumption by millions of gallons each day. This is a significant improvement over the original locks, which do not have water-saving features and require a full lock chamber of fresh water to be used and then released into the ocean for each ship that passes through.

In addition to the new locks, the expansion also involved widening and deepening the canal's navigation channels. This was necessary to allow larger ships to safely pass through the canal without running aground. The original canal's channels were not wide enough for two ships to pass each other in certain sections, and the depth of the channels was too shallow for the larger post-Panamax ships. As part of the expansion, engineers dredged the canal's channels to deepen them, and they widened certain parts of the canal to create passing lanes where two ships could navigate at the same time. This has made the canal much more efficient, as ships no longer have to wait as long for a clear passage through the narrower parts of the canal.

The expanded canal also required the construction of new access channels to connect the new locks with the rest of the canal. On the Pacific side, a new 3-mile-long (5-kilometer) access channel was built to link the new Cocolí Locks with the existing Gaillard Cut, the narrowest part of the canal. On the Atlantic side, a new access channel was created to connect the new Agua Clara Locks with Gatun Lake. These new channels were built with careful attention to environmental and safety concerns, as dredging and excavation work had the potential to disrupt the surrounding ecosystems and communities. The Panama Canal Authority worked closely with environmental experts to minimize the impact of the construction on wildlife and the local environment, and several programs were put in place to protect species like manatees, crocodiles, and fish that live in the canal's waters.

By the time the expanded canal opened in June 2016, the project had taken nine years to complete and had cost more than $5.4 billion. The expansion was officially inaugurated with the passage of a giant Chinese container ship, the Cosco Shipping Panama, through the new locks. The expanded canal immediately began handling post-Panamax ships, and its impact on global trade was felt almost immediately. Shipping companies were quick to take advantage of the larger canal, which allowed them to move more cargo in fewer trips, reducing costs and increasing efficiency. Many of the world's largest ports, particularly in the United States, Asia, and Latin America, also began upgrading their facilities to accommodate the larger ships that could now pass through the expanded canal.

The expansion of the Panama Canal has had a huge impact on global trade. Before the expansion, many of the world's largest ships, especially those carrying goods from Asia to the United States, had to take longer routes through the Suez Canal in Egypt or around the southern tip of South America. The expanded Panama Canal provides a much shorter and faster route, which has made trade between Asia and the Americas more efficient and cost-effective. For example, a ship traveling from Shanghai, China, to New York, USA, saves about 4,000 miles by using the Panama Canal instead of sailing around the southern tip of South America. This shorter route saves time, fuel, and money, which benefits not only the shipping companies but also the global economy.

In addition to benefiting trade between Asia and the Americas, the expanded canal has also had a major impact on trade within the Americas. Latin American countries, especially those in South America, have been able to take advantage of the expanded canal to increase their exports of goods like agricultural products, minerals, and oil. Brazil, for example, has used the expanded canal to ship more of its soybeans and other agricultural products to markets in Asia. Similarly, countries like Chile and Peru have benefited from being able to export more copper, iron ore, and other minerals through the expanded canal. This has strengthened economic ties between Latin America and Asia and has provided new opportunities for growth in the region.

The expansion of the Panama Canal has also had significant environmental benefits. By providing a shorter and more efficient route for shipping, the expanded canal has reduced the amount of fuel that ships need to burn, which has helped lower greenhouse gas emissions. This is especially important given the increasing concerns about climate change and the need to reduce the environmental impact of global trade. The water-saving basins in the new locks also help conserve one of Panama's most valuable resources—freshwater. By recycling water in the lock system, the expanded canal uses less water overall, which is crucial for maintaining the health of Panama's ecosystems and ensuring that the canal can continue to operate even during periods of drought.

However, the expansion of the Panama Canal has not been without its challenges. One of the biggest concerns has been the potential for increased traffic through the canal to strain Panama's infrastructure and environment. As more and larger ships pass through the canal, there is a greater risk of accidents, oil spills, and other environmental hazards. The Panama Canal Authority has put in place strict safety and environmental regulations to minimize these risks, but the potential for environmental damage remains a concern. Additionally, the expansion has led to increased competition between the Panama Canal and other major shipping routes, such as the Suez Canal and the northern sea routes through the Arctic. As global shipping patterns continue to evolve, it will be important for the Panama Canal to remain competitive and efficient to ensure its continued relevance in global trade.

In conclusion, the expansion of the Panama Canal has had a profound impact on global trade and the economy, allowing larger ships to pass through, reducing shipping times, and increasing efficiency. The expansion project was a massive engineering achievement that took nearly a decade to complete and involved numerous innovations, including the construction of new locks, access channels, and water-saving basins. The expanded canal has strengthened economic ties between countries around the world, especially between Asia and the Americas, and has helped reduce the environmental impact of shipping. Despite the challenges, the Panama Canal remains one of the most important waterways in the world, and its expansion has ensured that it will continue to play a vital role in global trade for many years to come.

Chapter 17: Life in Panama Before the Canal

Before the Panama Canal was built, life in Panama was very different from what it would become after this major engineering project was completed. Panama, which lies at the narrowest point between North and South America, was a relatively quiet and underdeveloped region in the late 1800s and early 1900s. It was a land of dense jungles, tropical rainforests, high mountains, and small towns. The people who lived there were mostly farmers, fishermen, and traders. They lived in small villages or scattered communities, and their lives were closely connected to the natural environment. There was no major international influence, no heavy industry, and no large-scale development. The story of life in Panama before the canal is one of simplicity, isolation, and a deep connection to the land and sea.

Panama was originally part of the larger region known as Gran Colombia, which included modern-day Colombia, Venezuela, Ecuador, and Panama. After gaining independence from Spain in the early 19th century, Panama became a part of Colombia in 1821. For much of the 19th century, Panama was a remote and somewhat forgotten region of Colombia. It was difficult to reach and travel across, with thick jungles, steep mountains, and swampland making it challenging for anyone to move from one side of the isthmus to the other. The Panama Railroad, which was completed in 1855, was the only real transportation link across the isthmus. It played an important role in connecting the Atlantic and Pacific Oceans, especially during the California Gold Rush when thousands of people crossed Panama on their way to the gold fields of California.

Despite the importance of the Panama Railroad, life in Panama remained relatively unchanged for most people. The economy was mostly agricultural, with small farms dotting the countryside. Farmers grew crops like bananas, sugarcane, coffee, and cacao, which they would sell in local markets or to traders passing through. Fishing was also an important part of the economy, particularly for the people living along the coasts. Fishermen would catch fish, shrimp, and other seafood, which they would sell or trade with their neighbors. Many Panamanians lived in simple homes made of wood, thatch, and other natural materials. Their lives were quiet and largely self-sufficient, with families growing their own food, making their own clothes, and trading goods with nearby villages.

The indigenous peoples of Panama, including the Kuna, Embera, and Wounaan, had lived in the region for thousands of years before the arrival of Europeans. These indigenous groups had their own distinct cultures, languages, and ways of life. They lived in harmony with the environment, relying on the land and rivers for food, medicine, and materials to build their homes. Their traditional knowledge of the forests and rivers helped them survive in the challenging environment of Panama's jungles. They would hunt, fish, and gather plants from the rainforest, and their communities were often organized around extended families. The Kuna people, for example, lived in villages along the Caribbean coast and the San Blas Islands, where they cultivated crops and engaged in fishing. The Kuna maintained their independence and resisted outside influences, even as Panama became more connected to the outside world.

For most people in Panama, travel and communication were slow and difficult before the canal. The region's geography made it hard to move from one side of the isthmus to the other. In addition to the Panama Railroad, people used small boats to navigate Panama's rivers and coasts, but these trips could be dangerous due to the unpredictable weather and the presence of wildlife like crocodiles and jaguars. There were few roads, and those that did exist were often little more than dirt paths that turned to mud during the rainy season. Travelers and traders who needed to cross the isthmus often faced long, exhausting journeys through the jungle, where they had to deal with insects, heat, and rain.

While Panama was a part of Colombia, its strategic location attracted attention from other countries. In particular, the United States and European nations recognized the importance of Panama as a possible route for a canal that would connect the Atlantic and Pacific Oceans. In the mid-1800s, several attempts were made to explore and survey the region for the construction of a canal. However, the jungle terrain, diseases like malaria and yellow fever, and the sheer difficulty of building such a project in such a remote area prevented any real progress.

In 1881, a French engineer named Ferdinand de Lesseps, who had successfully overseen the construction of the Suez Canal in Egypt, launched an ambitious project to build a canal across Panama. The French effort, however, quickly ran into serious problems. Workers faced terrible conditions, including extreme heat, torrential rains, and the constant threat of disease. Malaria and yellow fever, both of which are spread by mosquitoes, killed thousands of workers, and landslides often buried the construction sites under tons of mud and debris. The French eventually gave up on the project in 1889, leaving behind a legacy of failure, loss of life, and abandoned equipment. Life in Panama during this period was marked by hardship, as the failed canal project left many Panamanians struggling to survive in a land still isolated from the rest of the world.

For the indigenous people and local Panamanian communities, the French canal effort was an unsettling experience. The arrival of thousands of foreign workers and the French administrators brought new diseases, new cultural influences, and new social dynamics. The local economy was disrupted as workers were brought in from other countries, and the failure of the French project left the people of Panama with little to show for the effort. The French attempt also highlighted the challenges of living in a region where diseases like malaria and yellow fever were constant threats.

By the turn of the 20th century, Panama was still a mostly rural and isolated region, though its strategic importance remained clear. In 1903, Panama gained its independence from Colombia, with significant support from the United States. Shortly after Panama's independence, the United States took over the canal project, and life in Panama began to change rapidly. The U.S. brought in tens of thousands of workers from all over the world, including the Caribbean, Europe, Asia, and the United States itself. They established the Panama Canal Zone, a strip of land that stretched from coast to coast and was under U.S. control. The construction of the canal dramatically changed the social, economic, and physical landscape of Panama.

Before the arrival of the canal construction workers, Panama's population was relatively small, and the region was sparsely populated. The arrival of foreign workers changed the makeup of Panama's society, bringing with it new languages, customs, and ways of life. Many of the workers who came to build the canal, especially those from the Caribbean, stayed in Panama after the canal was completed, adding to the cultural diversity of the country. This marked the beginning of a new chapter in Panama's history, as the region moved from being a remote and largely forgotten part of Colombia to a key player in global trade and commerce.

The construction of the Panama Canal also brought new opportunities for economic growth, but it also introduced social tensions and inequality. While the canal project provided jobs for many people, the workforce was often divided along racial and social lines. Workers from the Caribbean, who were mostly Black, were paid lower wages and given harder, more dangerous jobs than their counterparts from the United States or Europe. This system of segregation, known as the "silver roll" and "gold roll," was a major source of resentment among the workers. The "gold roll" workers, who were mostly white Americans and Europeans, were paid in gold and given better living conditions, while the "silver roll" workers, who were mostly from the Caribbean and other non-white countries, were paid in silver and lived in poorer conditions.

Even though life in Panama was challenging before the canal was built, the arrival of the canal brought both positive and negative changes. For the people who lived in the region, the canal meant new opportunities for trade, work, and connection to the wider world. But it also brought foreign control, social division, and environmental changes. The lush jungles and rainforests that once covered much of Panama were cleared to make way for the canal, and the creation of Gatun Lake, the large artificial lake that supplies water for the canal, flooded vast areas of land, displacing people and wildlife.

The indigenous peoples of Panama, who had lived in the region for thousands of years before the arrival of Europeans, faced significant changes as well. Some indigenous groups were displaced from their traditional lands as the canal zone was established, and their way of life was disrupted by the arrival of foreign workers and new infrastructure. However, many indigenous people continued to live in the more remote parts of Panama, maintaining their traditional cultures and ways of life, even as the canal brought dramatic changes to the rest of the country.

In summary, life in Panama before the canal was one of simplicity and isolation. The people of Panama lived in small villages, farming, fishing, and trading to survive in a land of jungles and mountains. Travel was difficult, and communication with the outside world was limited. The indigenous peoples of Panama lived in harmony with the land, and their traditional cultures remained strong. The arrival of foreign interests, first with the French canal effort and later with the U.S. canal project, brought significant changes to Panama's economy, society, and environment. While the canal would eventually bring Panama into the center of global trade, life in the region before the

canal was a world apart, shaped by the rhythms of nature and the
challenges of living in a remote and rugged landscape.

83

Chapter 18: The Engineering Marvels of the Canal

The Panama Canal is one of the most incredible engineering marvels in human history. It stands as a symbol of human ingenuity, determination, and the ability to overcome nature's toughest obstacles. To understand why the canal is considered such a marvel, we have to look at the many amazing features and technologies that went into making this massive waterway possible. From the digging of deep channels through mountains and jungles to the creation of locks that lift and lower ships, every part of the Panama Canal is a triumph of engineering. This monumental project required creativity, bold ideas, and cutting-edge technology to solve problems that had never been tackled on such a scale before.

One of the most impressive aspects of the Panama Canal is the way it cuts through the Isthmus of Panama, a narrow strip of land that connects North and South America. When the idea of building the canal was first proposed, many people thought it was impossible. The land in Panama is not flat. Instead, it's full of dense rainforests, towering mountains, and deep valleys. In some places, the canal builders had to carve through rock-hard mountains, while in other areas they had to navigate through swamps filled with disease-carrying mosquitoes. The canal's designers and workers had to figure out how to create a waterway that could pass through this challenging landscape and connect the Atlantic and Pacific Oceans. They succeeded, but only after facing years of struggles, setbacks, and challenges.

One of the most important features of the canal is the lock system. The Panama Canal isn't just a straight waterway that runs at sea level from one ocean to the other. If it were, the engineers would have had to dig an impossibly deep and long trench across Panama. Instead, the canal uses locks to raise and lower ships as they travel from one ocean to the other. A lock is a kind of water-filled chamber that ships enter. Once inside the lock, water is either added to or drained from the chamber to raise or lower the ship to the next level of the canal. This system allows ships to climb over Panama's high hills and then be gently lowered back down on the other side. Without the locks, it would have been impossible to build the canal because the terrain of Panama is too varied.

There are three sets of locks along the canal: the Gatun Locks on the Atlantic side, the Pedro Miguel Locks, and the Miraflores Locks on the Pacific side. Each lock is made up of massive chambers, built to hold even the largest ships that sail the seas. In the original locks, which opened in 1914, these chambers were 110 feet wide, 1,000 feet long, and about 41 feet deep. When ships enter the locks, powerful gates close behind them to form a watertight seal. Then, the magic of the locks begins. Giant valves are opened to allow water to rush into the lock, raising the ship to the next level if it's moving uphill. If the ship is moving downhill, water is drained from the lock until the ship is lowered to the next level. Once the water levels are adjusted, the gates in front of the ship open, and the vessel moves forward to the next part of its journey.

The operation of the locks relies on gravity and a vast amount of freshwater, which comes from nearby rivers and lakes. The engineers who designed the canal made one of the most ingenious decisions when they chose to create Gatun Lake, an enormous artificial lake that provides the water necessary to operate the locks. Without Gatun Lake, the canal couldn't function because there wouldn't be enough water to fill the locks. Gatun Lake also serves as part of the waterway itself, so ships actually sail across the lake on their journey through the canal. The lake is one of the largest man-made lakes in the world, covering about 164 square miles (425 square kilometers), and it plays a crucial role in keeping the canal running smoothly.

The locks themselves are engineering wonders. The gates of the locks, which are made of steel, are incredibly heavy, each weighing as much as 750 tons. These gates are carefully designed to withstand the enormous pressure of the water behind them, and they are operated by electric motors that open and close them with precision. The original lock gates, despite their age, are still in use today, over 100 years after the canal first opened. These gates are divided into two sections that meet in the middle to create a tight seal, ensuring that no water can escape while the ship is being raised or lowered.

One of the biggest challenges in designing the locks was finding a way to move the ships through them without causing damage to the canal walls or the ships themselves. This led to the creation of the "mules," or electric locomotives, that guide the ships through the locks. These mules run on tracks along the sides of the locks, and their job is to pull and guide the ships, keeping them in the center of the lock chamber. The mules use steel cables to connect to the ships and ensure that they move smoothly through the locks without bumping into the walls or getting stuck. It's an incredible feat of engineering that these massive ships, sometimes weighing hundreds of thousands of tons, can be guided with such precision by the mules.

The creation of the Panama Canal also required some extraordinary feats of excavation. One of the toughest parts of building the canal was digging through the Culebra Cut, also known as the Gaillard Cut, which is a section of the canal that runs through the mountains of Panama. Here, workers had to dig through solid rock to create a channel deep enough and wide enough for ships to pass through. The amount of material that had to be removed was staggering—over 100 million cubic yards (about 76 million cubic meters) of earth and rock were dug out during the construction of the canal. This massive excavation effort involved thousands of workers and required the use of the most advanced machinery available at the time, including steam shovels, dynamite, and dredging equipment.

But digging through the mountains wasn't the only challenge. The builders also had to deal with the tropical environment of Panama, which included constant rain, landslides, and the threat of deadly diseases like malaria and yellow fever. Landslides were a constant problem in the Culebra Cut. Even after the canal opened, workers had to keep clearing the cut of debris that would slide down from the steep hillsides. These landslides often slowed down progress and sometimes buried equipment and workers, making it one of the most dangerous parts of the canal's construction.

Another incredible aspect of the Panama Canal is the engineering that went into controlling the flow of water through the canal. Because the canal is essentially a giant system of water elevators, managing the water supply is crucial. Engineers designed a series of spillways, dams, and reservoirs to control the flow of water from the surrounding rivers and lakes into the canal. One of the key structures in this system is the Gatun Dam, which holds back the Chagres River and creates Gatun Lake. The dam is a massive structure, over a mile long and 100 feet high (about 30 meters), and it was one of the largest earth dams in the world when it was built. The dam ensures that Gatun Lake stays full enough to provide the water needed for the locks, and it also helps control flooding during the rainy season.

The canal's expansion, which was completed in 2016, added even more impressive engineering feats to the waterway. The new, larger set of locks, called the "Third Set of Locks," allows for much bigger ships, known as Neo-Panamax vessels, to pass through the canal. These new locks are even wider, longer, and deeper than the original locks, and they include water-saving basins that help reduce the amount of water needed for each lockage. The new locks work in a similar way to the original ones, but they are designed to handle ships that are more than twice the size of those that could pass through the original locks. These Neo-Panamax ships can carry up to 14,000 containers, compared to about 5,000 containers on a Panamax ship. The expansion was a massive project in its own right, requiring new excavation work, new locks, and new access channels, all while keeping the original canal in operation.

The water-saving basins in the new locks are another example of the brilliant engineering behind the canal. These basins are designed to capture and reuse up to 60% of the water that would otherwise be lost when the locks are emptied. This is important because, even though Panama gets a lot of rain, managing the water supply for the canal is a constant challenge. The water-saving basins reduce the strain on Gatun Lake and help ensure that there is enough water to keep the canal running smoothly, even during dry periods.

In addition to the locks, the spillways, and the dams, the Panama Canal also features an impressive network of channels that guide ships through the waterway. These channels were carefully dredged and maintained to ensure that they are deep enough for ships to pass through safely. Dredging is an ongoing process at the canal because sediment from rivers and the surrounding landscape constantly flows into the waterway. Special dredging machines are used to remove this sediment and keep the canal's channels open. The channel that runs through Gatun Lake is one of the longest sections of the canal, and it's carefully maintained to ensure that ships can travel across the lake without running aground.

Another critical part of the canal's engineering is the traffic control system, which ensures that ships can pass through the canal efficiently and safely. Ships moving through the canal are guided by pilots—experienced captains who are familiar with the canal and its challenges. These pilots take control of the ships as they enter the canal and guide them through the locks and channels. The canal also has a series of traffic control centers, where engineers monitor the movement of ships using radar and communication systems. This allows the canal operators to manage the flow of traffic and ensure that ships move smoothly through the waterway without causing delays or accidents.

In conclusion, the Panama Canal is a true engineering marvel. It is not just a simple waterway but a complex system of locks, dams, spillways, channels, and control systems, all working together to make it possible for ships to cross from one ocean to the other. The technology behind the canal, from the massive lock gates to the electric locomotives that guide the ships, represents some of the most advanced engineering of its time. The expansion of the canal in recent years has added even more impressive features, allowing for larger ships to pass through and ensuring that the canal remains one of the most important trade routes in the world. The Panama Canal is a testament to the power of human creativity, determination, and the ability to overcome the greatest challenges nature can throw in our path.

Chapter 19: How the Canal Helps Ships Save Time

The Panama Canal is one of the most important shortcuts in the world for ships. It helps vessels save a huge amount of time by providing a much shorter and faster route between the Atlantic and Pacific Oceans. To understand how the canal saves time, it's helpful to think about what life was like for ships before the canal existed. Before the Panama Canal was completed in 1914, ships had to take a much longer and more dangerous journey to travel between the two oceans. They had to sail all the way around the southern tip of South America, through a region called Cape Horn, which was one of the longest and most treacherous sea routes in the world.

To get from the east coast of the United States, for example, to the west coast, ships would need to travel down the Atlantic Ocean, around the southernmost point of South America, and then back up the Pacific Ocean. This voyage was not only extremely long, often taking weeks or even months to complete, but it was also full of risks. Cape Horn is known for its fierce storms, rough seas, and dangerous winds, which made the journey very difficult for sailors. Many ships that attempted the journey around Cape Horn would be damaged or wrecked by the harsh conditions. It wasn't just bad weather that made the journey so hard—ships also had to deal with strong ocean currents, unpredictable icebergs, and the sheer distance of the trip.

The Panama Canal changed all of that. By cutting through the Isthmus of Panama, the canal created a direct water route between the Atlantic and Pacific Oceans that ships could use instead of going all the way around South America. The distance that ships have to travel was dramatically shortened. For example, the journey from New York City to San Francisco before the canal required a ship to sail about 13,000 miles (21,000 kilometers). After the canal was built, that distance was cut down to only about 5,200 miles (8,400 kilometers), less than half of the original distance. This shortcut meant that ships could reach their destinations much more quickly, saving weeks of travel time.

For ships traveling from Europe to the west coast of the Americas or from the west coast of the United States to Asia, the savings in time and distance were just as impressive. Without the Panama Canal, a ship traveling from Europe to the west coast of South America would have to sail south, pass through the Drake Passage, which lies between Cape Horn and Antarctica, and then head north again. This route not only added thousands of miles to the journey but also exposed ships to some of the roughest waters in the world. The Panama Canal provides a much safer and faster alternative. Instead of taking the long, dangerous trip around the southern tip of the continent, ships can simply pass through the narrow canal and be on their way in just a few hours.

One of the reasons the canal is so effective at saving time is because of how efficiently it operates. Ships can pass through the canal in about 8 to 10 hours, compared to the weeks it would take to sail around South America. The process of moving a ship through the canal begins when the ship arrives at one of the entrances, either on the Atlantic side or the Pacific side. From there, canal pilots, who are experts at navigating the waterway, take control of the ship and guide it through the system of locks and channels. The ship is raised and lowered by the locks as it moves through the canal, and it eventually emerges on the other side, ready to continue its journey.

This quick and efficient transit through the canal allows ships to reach their destinations much faster, which is especially important for the global shipping industry. Ships are used to transport all kinds of goods around the world, from food and raw materials to manufactured products and fuel. By saving time, the Panama Canal helps reduce the cost of shipping goods because ships can make more trips in a shorter amount of time. This efficiency is important for keeping the global economy running smoothly. When goods can be transported quickly and cheaply, it helps businesses operate more effectively and ensures that people around the world have access to the products they need.

In addition to saving time for individual ships, the Panama Canal plays a critical role in global trade by helping major shipping routes operate more efficiently. Many of the world's busiest shipping routes pass through the Panama Canal, including those between the east coast of the United States and Asia, and between Europe and the west coast of South America. By providing a shortcut, the canal allows shipping companies to plan their routes more effectively, saving time and fuel, which also helps to lower costs.

Fuel is a big part of why saving time on a journey is so important for ships. When ships take shorter routes, they burn less fuel, which makes their voyages more economical. The cost of fuel is one of the biggest expenses for shipping companies, so anything that helps reduce the amount of fuel a ship needs to use can make a big difference. Before the Panama Canal was built, ships that had to travel around South America used a lot of fuel because of the long distance and the challenging weather conditions. By allowing ships to take a much shorter route, the canal helps them save a significant amount of fuel, which is better for the environment and for the companies operating the ships.

Another important reason why the Panama Canal saves time is that it allows ships to avoid the dangers of the open ocean. Sailing around Cape Horn is not only a long and difficult journey but also a dangerous one. Ships traveling around the southern tip of South America face powerful storms, rough seas, and dangerous winds that can make the trip slow and hazardous. These harsh conditions can delay a ship's journey by days or even weeks. The Panama Canal offers a much safer and more predictable route. Ships traveling through the canal don't have to worry about ocean storms or icebergs. Instead, they can pass through the canal's calm waters in a matter of hours, without the risk of getting caught in bad weather.

The canal's ability to save time is not just important for commercial ships; it also helps military vessels move more quickly between the Atlantic and Pacific Oceans. In times of war or emergency, being able to move military ships quickly can make a huge difference. The Panama Canal allows naval ships to cross between the two oceans without having to take the long journey around South America, which gives countries with a presence in both the Atlantic and Pacific faster access to their fleets. This strategic importance has made the Panama Canal a vital part of the global military landscape.

The Panama Canal's recent expansion, which was completed in 2016, has made it even more effective at saving time for modern ships. The expansion added a new set of locks that are wider, longer, and deeper than the original ones, allowing larger ships, known as Neo-Panamax vessels, to pass through the canal. These ships can carry more cargo than the smaller Panamax ships that used to be the largest vessels able to pass through the canal. With the expanded canal, shipping companies can now move larger loads through the waterway, saving even more time and money. The expansion has allowed the canal to continue playing a vital role in global trade, especially as the size of cargo ships continues to grow.

Saving time is especially important for certain types of goods that need to be transported quickly. Perishable goods, like fruits, vegetables, and other food items, need to reach their destination before they spoil. Before the Panama Canal existed, transporting these kinds of goods around South America was a risky proposition because the long journey increased the chances that the food would spoil before it arrived. Today, the canal makes it possible for ships carrying perishable goods to take a much faster route, ensuring that food stays fresh and can be delivered to markets around the world more reliably.

The Panama Canal also helps save time for oil tankers and other ships carrying important natural resources like coal, iron ore, and grains. These resources are essential for industries around the world, and the faster they can be transported, the better. For example, oil tankers traveling from the Gulf of Mexico to Asia no longer have to make the long journey around South America. Instead, they can pass through the Panama Canal and deliver their cargo in a fraction of the time. This not only helps the oil industry operate more efficiently but also ensures that countries around the world have access to the energy resources they need.

Beyond helping individual ships save time, the Panama Canal also has a big impact on the global economy as a whole. By reducing the time it takes to transport goods, the canal helps keep the cost of products down. When goods can be moved quickly and efficiently, businesses don't have to spend as much money on transportation, and these savings can be passed on to consumers. For example, a company that imports electronics from Asia can get its products to the United States or Europe much faster by using the Panama Canal. This means the company can sell its products at a lower price, which benefits consumers.

The canal's ability to save time also makes it easier for companies to manage their supply chains. In today's world, many businesses rely on just-in-time shipping, where products and materials are delivered exactly when they are needed. This allows companies to avoid keeping large amounts of inventory in storage, which saves money. The Panama Canal plays a key role in just-in-time shipping because it allows goods to be transported quickly and reliably between different parts of the world. By helping ships save time, the canal makes it possible for businesses to operate more efficiently and keep their products moving through the global marketplace.

In conclusion, the Panama Canal is an incredible time-saving shortcut for ships traveling between the Atlantic and Pacific Oceans. By providing a much shorter route, the canal allows ships to avoid the long and dangerous journey around Cape Horn, cutting weeks off their travel time. The canal's locks, channels, and efficient operation make it possible for ships to pass through in just a few hours, further reducing the time it takes to transport goods around the world. This saves fuel, lowers costs, and helps keep the global economy running smoothly. The Panama Canal continues to be one of the most important and impressive engineering achievements, making global trade faster, safer, and more efficient.

Chapter 20: The Future of the Panama Canal

The Panama Canal is one of the greatest engineering marvels in the world and has been essential to global trade for over a century. Its impact on the movement of goods and ships between the Atlantic and Pacific Oceans is immense, but the future of the Panama Canal is equally fascinating. Over the years, the canal has evolved to meet the demands of modern shipping, and it will continue to play a critical role in world trade. However, challenges such as the increasing size of ships, environmental concerns, technological advancements, and the potential for new shipping routes will all influence what happens to the canal in the future. The canal's future is full of exciting possibilities, with many factors that could shape its path forward.

One of the most important aspects of the future of the Panama Canal is how it will continue to accommodate the growing size of ships. As global trade has expanded, so has the size of the vessels used to transport goods. The ships that sail through the canal today are much larger than those that passed through when it first opened in 1914. In response to this, the canal underwent a major expansion, which was completed in 2016. This expansion added a new set of locks, called the Neo-Panamax locks, which are wider, deeper, and longer than the original locks. These new locks can handle much larger ships, known as Neo-Panamax vessels, which can carry three times more cargo than the older Panamax ships. This expansion was a major success, allowing more ships to pass through and ensuring that the canal remained competitive with other shipping routes.

However, ship sizes continue to grow, and there are now vessels that are even larger than the Neo-Panamax ships. These ships, known as Ultra Large Container Vessels (ULCVs), are too big to fit through the Panama Canal, even after the expansion. This presents a challenge for the future of the canal, as more shipping companies are building larger ships to carry more cargo and reduce transportation costs. One option for the future might be another expansion of the canal to accommodate these massive vessels. However, this would require a significant investment of time and money, and it would also raise concerns about the environmental impact of further construction. While it is possible that the canal could be expanded again, it is also possible that shipping companies will continue to rely on smaller vessels that can fit through the current locks, balancing the need for efficiency with the constraints of the canal.

Another important factor in the future of the Panama Canal is its environmental impact. The canal plays a vital role in global trade, but operating such a massive infrastructure project has significant environmental consequences. The construction of the canal dramatically altered the landscape of Panama, affecting local ecosystems and wildlife. The expansion in 2016 also had environmental impacts, including the need to use large amounts of water to operate the new locks. Freshwater from Gatun Lake is used to fill the locks and raise and lower ships as they pass through, and each time a ship moves through the canal, millions of gallons of water are released into the ocean. This demand for water has led to concerns about the sustainability of the canal, especially as climate change and shifting weather patterns affect the availability of freshwater.

As global temperatures rise, the Panama Canal is facing new challenges from droughts and changing rainfall patterns. Gatun Lake, which supplies the canal with water, relies on rainfall to stay full. In recent years, Panama has experienced periods of drought, which has lowered water levels in the lake and made it harder to supply the locks with the necessary amount of water. If water levels in the lake continue to drop, it could limit the number of ships that can pass through the canal or force the canal to restrict the size of ships that can be accommodated. To address this challenge, the Panama Canal

Authority is exploring new ways to conserve water and make the canal more efficient. One possibility is to develop new water-saving technologies that would reduce the amount of water needed to operate the locks. Another option might be to create additional reservoirs or water storage systems to ensure a steady supply of water for the canal. These efforts will be critical in ensuring that the canal can continue to function effectively in the face of changing environmental conditions.

Technological advancements are another exciting area that will shape the future of the Panama Canal. As technology continues to improve, the canal could become even more efficient and capable of handling larger numbers of ships. For example, advances in automation and robotics could allow the canal to operate more smoothly and with fewer delays. Currently, the canal relies on a combination of human operators and mechanical systems to guide ships through the locks and channels. However, in the future, it is possible that many of these tasks could be automated, allowing ships to pass through the canal more quickly and with less human intervention. Drones, sensors, and artificial intelligence could also be used to monitor the condition of the canal's infrastructure, detect maintenance needs, and improve the overall efficiency of the waterway.

In addition to technological improvements, the future of the Panama Canal will also be shaped by changes in global trade patterns. The world's shipping routes are constantly evolving as new markets emerge, and changes in trade agreements, supply chains, and geopolitical relationships can have a significant impact on which routes are most important. For example, the rise of manufacturing in Asia and increased trade between the Americas and Asia has made the Panama Canal an essential part of many shipping routes. However, other developments, such as the expansion of the Suez Canal or the possibility of new Arctic shipping routes opening up due to melting ice, could affect the future importance of the Panama Canal.

The Arctic route, in particular, presents an interesting challenge for the Panama Canal. As global temperatures rise and Arctic ice melts, it may become possible for ships to travel through the Arctic Ocean during the summer months. This route would be much shorter for ships traveling between Europe and Asia, potentially saving even more time than the Panama Canal. However, the Arctic route also comes with significant challenges, including unpredictable weather, ice, and environmental concerns. While it is unlikely that the Arctic route will fully replace the Panama Canal, it could become a viable alternative for some shipping companies, especially those looking to reduce their travel time and fuel costs.

Despite these challenges, the Panama Canal is likely to remain one of the most important shipping routes in the world for the foreseeable future. The canal has proven itself to be adaptable, with expansions and improvements that have kept it competitive in the face of changing global trade patterns. The recent expansion has allowed the canal to handle larger ships, and ongoing investments in technology and infrastructure will help it continue to play a critical role in world trade.

The canal's importance extends beyond just shipping, however. It is also a vital part of Panama's economy and national identity. The revenue generated by the canal is a significant source of income for the Panamanian government, and the canal's operation provides jobs for thousands of people. As Panama continues to develop, the canal will remain a key driver of economic growth, attracting international investment and helping to support the country's broader economic development goals.

In addition to its economic importance, the Panama Canal has a symbolic significance that goes beyond its role as a transportation route. The canal is a symbol of human ingenuity and determination, a testament to the ability of people to overcome incredible challenges and create something that changes the world. This legacy will continue to inspire future generations as they work to address the challenges of the 21st century, from climate change to technological innovation.

One of the most exciting possibilities for the future of the Panama Canal is the potential for further innovation in the way it is used. As shipping companies look for ways to reduce their environmental impact, there is growing interest in the use of alternative fuels, such as hydrogen, ammonia, and electricity, to power ships. These cleaner fuels could help reduce the carbon footprint of global shipping, and the Panama Canal could play a role in supporting this transition. The canal's strategic location makes it an ideal spot for refueling stations that provide ships with access to alternative fuels. In the future, the canal could become a hub for green shipping, helping to reduce the environmental impact of the global supply chain.

There is also the potential for the canal to be used for purposes beyond shipping. For example, the canal could play a role in the development of new industries, such as offshore wind energy or deep-sea mining. The waters around Panama are rich in natural resources, and the canal's location makes it an ideal gateway for companies looking to explore these opportunities. As the global economy continues to evolve, the Panama Canal could become a central part of new and emerging industries, helping to drive economic growth and innovation in the region.

In conclusion, the future of the Panama Canal is full of possibilities. The canal has already proven itself to be one of the most important and enduring infrastructure projects in the world, and it will continue to play a vital role in global trade for many years to come. As the size of ships increases, the canal may need to undergo further expansions, but it will also benefit from advances in technology and efforts to reduce its environmental impact. Climate change, new shipping routes, and changing trade patterns will all shape the future of the canal, but it is well-positioned to adapt to these challenges. As the world continues to change, the Panama Canal will remain a critical part of the global economy, helping to connect people and goods across the world while also serving as a symbol of human ingenuity and resilience.

Epilogue

Now that you've explored the fascinating history of the Panama Canal, you've seen how an ambitious dream became a reality through teamwork, ingenuity, and determination. From the first bold ideas to the final stones laid, the Panama Canal has remained one of the most important engineering achievements in the world.

But the story of the Panama Canal doesn't end here. Even today, the canal continues to evolve. With larger ships crossing the oceans and global trade increasing, the Panama Canal has expanded and adapted to meet modern needs. It stands as a reminder of what humans can achieve when faced with tough challenges.

As you grow, there may be even bigger engineering projects to solve new problems in our world. Who knows? Maybe you'll be part of the next big idea that changes the way people live and connect.

The Panama Canal is more than just a shortcut; it's proof that when we think big, we can make the impossible possible. And as the canal continues to shape the future, it will inspire future generations—just like you—to dream, build, and make their own mark on the world.

The End.